Spitfire Command

Titles in the 'Fortunes of War' series

ALERT IN THE WEST
A Luftwaffe Pilot on the Western Front

ARK ROYAL

BETRAYED IDEALS
Memoirs of a Luftwaffe Fighter Ace

BLACK SATURDAY
The Royal Oak Tragedy at Scapa Flow

CAMBRAI
The First Tank Battle

CONVOY COMMODORE

DARK SEAS ABOVE
HM Submarine Taurus

DEFEAT OF THE WOLF PACKS

ENEMY IN THE DARK
The Story of a Night-Fighter Pilot

FAITH, HOPE & CHARITY
The Defence of Malta

FLY FOR YOUR LIFE
The Story of Bob Stanford Tuck

GALLIPOLI 1915

GINGER LACEY
Fighter Ace

HMS ILLUSTRIOUS
The Fight for Life

HMS WARSPITE
The Story of a Famous Battleship

LAUGHING COW
The Story of U69

LIGHTNING STRIKES
The Story of a B-17 Bomber

MANNOCK, VC
Ace With One Eye

MUSTANG ACE
The Story of Don S Gentile

ONE OF THE FEW
A Triumphant Story of Combat in the Battle of Britain

OPERATION BARBAROSSA

PHANTOM RAIDER
Nazi Germany's Most Successful Surface Raider

PRINZ EUGEN
The Graceful Predator

RELENTLESS PURSUIT
The Story of Captain F J Walker, CB, DSO★★★, RN

RICHTHOFEN
The Red Knight of the Air

SPITFIRE ATTACK

STALINGRAD
Enemy at the Gates

THE BATTLE OF THE ARDENNES

THE BATTLE OF THE ATLANTIC

THE FIRST AND THE LAST
Germany's Fighter Force in WWII

THE GREAT INVASION
The Roman Conquest of Britain

THE LAST VOYAGE OF THE GRAF SPEE

THE MIGHTY HOOD
The Life & Death of the Royal Navy's Proudest Ship

THE MOUCHOTTE DIARIES

THE SINKING OF THE BISMARCK
The Death of a Flagship

THE SINKING OF THE SCHARNHORST
The German Account

THE SOMME
Death of a Generation

TIRPITZ
Pride of the Kriegsmarine

TOBRUK
The Story of a Siege

U-BOAT 977
The U-Boat That Escaped to Argentina

U-BOAT ACES

U-BOAT COMMANDER
The Story of Günther Prien

YPRES
Death of an Army

FORTUNES OF WAR

Spitfire Command

BY GROUP CAPTAIN BOBBY OXSPRING DFC**, AFC

CERBERUS

First published by William Kimber & Co Ltd in 1984

PUBLISHED IN THE UNITED KINGDOM BY;

Cerberus Publishing Limited

Penn House

Leigh Woods

Bristol BS8 3PF, United Kingdom

Tel: ++44 (0) 117 974 7175

Fax: ++44 (0) 117 973 0890

e-mail: cerberusbooks@aol.com

www.cerberbus-publishing.com

British Library Cataloguing in Publication Data.
A catalogue record for this book is available from the British Library.

ISBN 1 84145 033 2

PRINTED AND BOUND IN MALTA.

Contents

Acknowledgements   6

Foreword by Air Vice-Marshal 'Johnnie' Johnson, CB, CBE, DSO, DFC, DL.   8

Introduction   10

CHAPTER ONE   FATHER'S FOOTSTEPS   12

CHAPTER TWO   'PREPARE FOR WAR'   20

CHAPTER THREE   'KEEP IT ON THE AIRFIELD'   28

CHAPTER FOUR   'WE SHALL NEVER SURRENDER'   40

CHAPTER FIVE   'GET IT RIGHT, OLD BOY'   47

CHAPTER SIX   'DON'T PANIC, I'VE GOT 'EM SURROUNDED!'   55

CHAPTER SEVEN   'THERE THEY GO'   68

CHAPTER EIGHT   'BACK, CHAPS, WE'RE IN THE SHIT'   77

CHAPTER NINE   'LET'S FACE IT!'   88

CHAPTER TEN   'IT LOOKS A BIT DICEY'   98

CHAPTER ELEVEN   'A STRIP OF WIRE NETTIN''   108

CHAPTER TWELVE   'A FIGHTER PILOT'S BREAKFAST'   117

CHAPTER THIRTEEN   'POSTED TO HEADQUARTERS'   128

CHAPTER FOURTEEN   'IF I DON'T GET LEAVE SOON'   138

CHAPTER FIFTEEN   'A COUPLE OF CHATTERING WRECKS'   145

Appendix: Combat record   154

Bibliography   156

Index   157

Acknowledgements

In the writing of this book I have been much encouraged by my family, friends and former colleagues whose generous contributions have helped to keep the record straight, especially when the long span of years since World War II tend to fade the memory.

For his elegant foreword, I am indebted to Air Vice Marshal Johnnie Johnson whose matchless combat record in the wartime skies was a continuing inspiration to his fellow fighter pilots.

Had it not been for the generous contribution of Mrs Gill Gornford in typing the manuscript, it is doubtful if it would ever have been finished. Her home being in West Germany made communication between us difficult at times, but somehow she overcame all obstacles and I extend to her my abiding gratitude.

My sincere thanks also go to:

Air Chief Marshal Sir John Barraclough KCB, CBE, DFC, AFC

Air Marshal Sir Edward Chilton KBE, CB

Air Commodore A I Winskill CBE, DFC

Wing Commander D G S R Cox, DFC

General Adolph Galland

Leutnant Erich Bodendiek

Flying Officer Chris Goss RAF

Mr Alfred Price FR Hist. S

Mr Michael McCaul CMG

Mr and Mrs Dale Parkinson

Mr Malcom Smith

Flight Sergeant Kerry Leveson HNC

Mr Peter Gill

Mrs Helen Sears

Dr T Smatlhorn

Mrs Betty Lardner-Burke

I tender my appreciation to the staffs of the Imperial War Museum and the College Library at Royal Air Force, Cranwell for their valuable assistance.

Foreword

by Air Vice-Marshal 'Johnnie' Johnson
CB, CBE, DSO (Two Bars), DFC (And Bar), DL

Apart from two brief 'rests' from operational flying, Group Captain 'Bobby' Oxspring, DFC and two Bars, was one of that select band of fighter pilots who flew throughout the Second World War, and in his excellent book he writes of the splendid characters he knew in the fighter squadrons.

The author relates that during the Battle of Britain the Germans had several advantages. They had a superiority of nearly three to one in aeroplanes and their Messerschmitt 109E was as good as our Spitfire I. As the aggressors they held the initiative and they could launch attacks from their airfields stretching from Norway to Brittany, which meant that Fighter Command had to separate its thin cover to defend many possible targets. Their fighter pilots, having fought in the Spanish Civil War and in the *Blitzkrieg* campaigns, had more combat experience than the pilots of Fighter Command.

With all these advantages, why did not the Germans win? Basically, it was because we had radar and the essential warning it provided, excellent commanders, and a short chain of command from Dowding to the group commanders, to the station and squadron commanders, and to the fighter pilots of whom the author writes.

What sort of men were they? Some of them were straight from school and were very young. Others, like Douglas Bader and 'Sailor' Malan, from South Africa, were nearly thirty, and some of the superb Poles and Czechs were older still. There were week-end pilots from the Royal Air Force Volunteer Reserve, and there were the well-publicised 'long-haired' Auxiliary Squadrons who were generally up to the standards of their regular comrades.

They were quick, responsive, proud, highly-strung, young in years – twenty-five was maturity and thirty was old-age - and brought to near perfection a form of warfare invented, as the author relates, by their fathers. Probably the secret of their success was that they were ordinary men who, when the call came, rose to extra-ordinary heights. In the words of the poem, the average Battle of Britain pilot was;

> 'A common, unconsidered man who, for a moment of
> eternity, held the whole future of mankind in
> his two sweating palms – *and did not let it fall.*'

Introduction

Following the precedent set by the Royal Flying Corps in the Great War, the Royal Air Force continued to enlist aircrew from all parts of the Commonwealth. Nearly every squadron had staunch Empire representatives on its strength, and nowhere was this more true than in the fighter fraternity. In the early phases of World War II, as the Nazi steamroller occupied most European countries, an increasing number of those nationals who rejected subservience to the Teutonic heel escaped to Britain to continue the fight for liberation of their homelands. Many of these characters had flying experience and were welcomed by the Royal Air Force which was desperately short of trained crews, especially pilots.

Though predominantly British, the wartime RAF was composed of personalities from nearly every democratic country in the world. Never did a more courageous, competent and cavalier company assemble to defend the cause of freedom. I felt honoured to be accepted among them.

Each year, or on posting, it was mandatory that every pilot be assessed on his flying ability by his squadron commander, and the category attained of 'exceptional', 'above average', 'average' or 'below average' entered in his log book. The gifted few in the 'exceptional' class such as Johnson, Malan, Pattle and Tuck achieved admirable scores in kills against the enemy, but they would be the first to admit that their successes could not have been attained without the dedicated support of the 'average squadron pilots',

It is impossible to classify such characters, since by the definition of 'average', it is axiomatic that there must also be an equal number of 'below average' as 'above average'. Yet I never knew a fighter squadron commander throughout the war who admitted to having a 'below average' pilot on his strength. When it was evident that certain individuals couldn't cut the mustard they were quickly removed, not only from the squadron, but the command as well.

Thus, the vast numbers of 'average squadron pilots', to use the terminology of the day, soldiered on, often through two or three tours of operations. Their utter dependability, dedication and discipline shone in their unspectacular roles as wingmen and section leaders. In terms of enemy kills many achieved no more than one or two, yet their collective contribution far exceeded those of the established aces.

Countless courageous acts performed in the turbulent wartime skies remain unheralded. I have tried in this book to rectify some of these omissions, and to record some of the admirable feats of our unsung 'average' pilots which in many cases I was privileged to witness. I have relied heavily on copies of my combat reports, entries in my log book, and reminders from an old scrapbook. I have cross-checked incidents with numerous publications to establish the accuracy of the occasions, but the memory of the more spectacular events will never fade.

I have occasionally used phraseology which was not in vogue at the time, but which has since entered the air force vocabulary. In most cases they are more apt descriptions and I make no apology for them. I would prefer for instance to 'fall off the perch' than to 'initiate a high quarter attack', or perform 'an Immelmann' (so named after its WWI inaugurator) than 'a roll off the top of a loop'.

CHAPTER ONE

FATHER'S FOOTSTEPS

During my schooldays our family lived on the edge of the steel-manufacturing city of Sheffield. Wardsend, our ancient farmhouse, nestled near the shadow of the Wednesday football stadium which lay on the city's northern outskirts before the spread of the region's built-up area. The great industrial depression of the twenties and thirties hit us along with millions of others and money was tight. Not even the accolade of his election to the elite office of Master Cutler accorded to my maternal grandfather, Marmaduke Wardlow, in any way relieved the financial situation. Consequently, any aspirations I had of attending public school or of entry to the Royal Air Force College at Cranwell were doomed from the outset. At the same time, the aviation world was advancing with prodigious strides. As a result of three successive victories, Britain won the Schneider Trophy outright. The world speed, altitude and distance records fell to British pilots and aircraft. They were heady days for a youngster and the desire to fly became an obsession with me.

Once a year the Sheffield smog was penetrated by Alan Cobham's air circus. His barnstorming pilots made light of the gloom, and for two stirring days the intractable citizens of South Yorkshire moved fleetingly into the twentieth century. Open cockpit passenger flights were to be had for five shillings a trip and I made sure I got my ration. Short as the flights were, no more than a wide circuit and bump, they were exhilarating enough to whet my appetite for more. With the decade's wealth of aviation literature emerged a best-selling author in Captain W E Johns. His eagerly awaited novels centred on an intrepid hero called Biggles whose origins sprang from the incomparable Royal Flying Corps of the First World War. To me my father was my Biggles although his flying recollections were shorn of the more capricious antics of Johns' famous character.

In 1915 the necessity for military aviation at the front significantly increased. Expansion of the Flying Corps was a prerequisite and the demand for aircrews became urgent. Hence the primary recruitment devolved on the army regiments of the time.

Intrigued by the challenge of flight and disenchanted with the squalor of trench warfare through the previous winter, my father responded to the call for volunteers and his application for transfer from the King's Own Yorkshire Light Infantry was accepted.

The Flying Corps' requirements in 1915 decreed that he should be an observer and as such he was posted directly to No 12 Squadron. For several months he undertook the duties of reporting enemy troop concentrations and directing artillery fire. This brought basic air experience which later on was to prove invaluable to him. He continued to press for pilot training and finally it was granted.

The air experience gained as an observer, or 'sandbag' as he put it, on the BE 2c's of 12 Squadron must have undoubtedly helped in dispersing many uncertainties or ill-conceived notions about the basic mysteries of flying. Nevertheless it was no mean feat at Upavon to be permitted to fly solo on a Maurice Farman Shorthorn after only 1-hour and 15-minutes of dual instruction. From then on the training progressed smoothly and, having attained a total of some ten hours he gained his pilot's wings brevet. To his great delight he was posted to No 54 Squadron, then forming at Castle Bromwich near Birmingham, and thus became a founder member.

'Fifty-four' was the first RFC Squadron to be equipped with that famous little single-seat fighter the Sopwith Pup. Fighters in those days were known as 'Scouts' and to his dying day my father never referred to them as anything else. Squadron training proceeded as rapidly as possible and not without incident. My father's first solo in a Pup must surely rate as the shortest Flight on record. He was authorised for this trip one blustery day when the wind was most unpredictable, so much so that on taxi-ing out before take-off, the aircraft had to be steadied and prevented from weather-cocking by a couple of airmen holding each wing tip. Having thus manoeuvred to the take-off point, my father waved the airmen away and opened up the engine. Unfortunately there were no means of doing this gently since on a Pup there were only two throttle positions, maximum power and tick over. The combination of the suddenly applied power, the gusty wind, the powerful light controls especially alter the heavy Maurice Farman, and not least by the lack of restraining influence of the airmen, all added up to the Pup becoming airborne with no take-off run whatsoever.

In a few short seconds the aircraft and its very surprised pilot had performed a half loop and landed upside down some ten yards further back from the take-off point. My father maintained that in such an inverted predicament, some three feet from the ground and supported only by the harness, there was a problem in deciding how to release the straps without dropping out on his head and breaking his neck. However, the problem was solved and he was extracted intact. The overall crash damage fortunately was slight and both pilot and aircraft were serviceable again next day when a more prolonged and conventional flight was performed without incident.

'Fifty-Four' arrived in France on Christmas Eve 1916. It was the first squadron in Flanders to be equipped with Sopwith Pups which were to become the 'Spitfires' of the First World War. Until the advent of the Camel a year later, the Pups were the only Allied aircraft whose performance could match the current German machines. They became renowned for their lightness on controls, their manoeuvrability and their ability to climb and to maintain very high altitudes.

'Fifty-Four' joined the original aerial struggles to attain air superiority. After two years of war both sides had finally recognised the power of aircraft operating over the battlefield. The air war hotted up, and the names of early ace combat pilots such as Albert Ball and Max Immelmann became known. Basic fighter combat tactics were evolved which remained fundamentally unchanged up to the end of the Korean War.

The superior fighting qualities of the Pups of 'Fifty-Four' began to take effect, and as the tally of successful combats steadily mounted, the squadron's casualty list remained surprisingly small. Because of their ability to fight at altitude the Pups were frequently assigned as cover for reconnaissance and bomber squadrons operating over targets behind the German lines. It was on one of these missions that my father scored his first kill. He fastened on to the tail of a Rumpler two seater which tried to interfere with the raid, and opened fire. The enemy aircraft flicked into a spin in which after several turns it shed a mainplane and crashed near Bapaume.

Operating at altitudes of over seventeen thousand feet, apart from the lack of oxygen at such heights, the pilots in their open unheated cockpits were subjected to sub-zero temperatures where the danger of frostbite was ever present. Apart from the heavy fleece-lined flying coats and thigh-length boots, the aviators had to protect their faces with thick layers of whale grease under their goggles and scarves. They were rugged characters to subject themselves to such a toilette an hour before dawn on a winter's morning.

Perhaps it would be overstating the obvious to remark that the really great fighter aces were supreme marksmen. Most pilots could be taught with practice to shoot tolerably well, but the select few had a natural reaction to a moving target, and whatever the target's speed and position they could instantly and accurately assess the deflection required for a hit. This ability in the air was almost always reflected on the ground, and such pilots were excellent shots with a twelve bore against game birds or clay pigeons. My father had this ability to shoot accurately with any weapon and it stood him in good stead in the six months he flew as a scout pilot on the Western Front. He is recorded in the Harborough publication of *Air Aces of the 1914-1918 War* as being credited with sixteen German aircraft destroyed – not a startling total perhaps, but certainly commendable.

In April 1917 'Fifty-Four' moved from Bertangles, near Amiens, some 50-kms east to a new base at Flez where it took part in the battle of Arras. About this time my father was awarded a Bar to the Military Cross he had won with the KOYLI's. Later the following month he was promoted to flight commander, and posted to No 66 Squadron, also armed with Pups, to command B flight. With the change in squadrons came a change in fortunes, and the end of his flying career.

Separated from his formation in a dog fight during the Battle of Messines, he returned one June evening across the lines towards his base. The sun was beginning to set into a fairly thick haze rendering forward visibility almost zero. It appears that a Bristol Fighter was climbing in the opposite direction with its forward and upward visibility obscured by the top mainplane. By a million to one chance the two aircraft collided almost head on. As the aircraft cannoned off each other the Bristol Fighter took with it the majority of the lower port mainplane of my father's Pup. The collision occurred at about 4,000-feet and both crippled planes fell away into spins. In those days aircrew were not equipped with parachutes and many crews when faced with petrol fire in the air preferred to jump to death rather than be burnt alive. Just before the end of the Bristol Fighter's fatal spin to the ground, the aircraft burst into flames and both pilot and observer were killed.

Meanwhile my father spiralled down in a lopsided spin unable to control the machine in any way, and became resigned to a fate which daily claimed many men. Nearing the ground the Pup's crazy gyrations became momentarily more horizontal than vertical. Sensing that he was going to strike the ground one wing first at a fairly shallow tangent, my father snapped off the safety belt catch, held a centre strut and hung all his body out of the cockpit on the side away from the impending crash. Just before the wing hit the ground the wheels of the Pup ploughed into the top of a French haystack which cushioned the blow and cartwheeled the aircraft on to the ground. The impact forced the engine back into the cockpit carrying my father's legs with it almost into the rear fuselage. The force of the crash knocked him unconscious. When he came to a few minutes later he found himself soaked in petrol, impaled by his legs in the strewn wreckage and being extricated by willing Tommies who had appeared on the scene. One who offered him a cigarette must have been surprised at the emphatic refusal until it was suggested that they all get smartly away from the scattered petrol before playing around with fire.

A centre section strut from the crashed aircraft was used as a splint for my father's legs and he was carted off to a hospital in St Omer. Both legs were badly broken in several places but fortunately no amputation was necessary. After a painful year in hospitals all over England, he returned to light duties in London. Before he could walk properly without the aid of sticks, World War I was over. These frightful injuries prevented him from reaching the physical standard required to continue to serve as a regular officer. But in spite of it all his heart was still with the Air Force.

My father was one of that pioneering bunch of adventurers who created the art of warfare in the third element. In doing so they laid down the foundations of air power and it is not surprising that at the same time a service demanding different conceptions, applications and attitudes should be born too. War in the air exerts its peculiar demands, and to meet them the early aviators brought a new brand of skill and judgement. With them came an environment of mutual understanding which provided the guidelines to their successors in the sphere of military aviation. Air power in warfare had proved to be indispensable. Despite intense opposition from the two senior services the Royal Flying Corps was amalgamated with the Royal Naval Air Service. On 1 April 1918 the Royal Air Force was born and became the world's first air force completely independent of army and navy. That it did so was largely due to the remarkable foresight of Lord Trenchard (who became known as the father of the RAF), the resolution and clear-sighted planning of General Jan Smuts, and last but not least the unswerving support of Winston Churchill.

During the inter-war years successive governments sought stringent economic cuts largely by paring the fighting services to the bone. This short-sighted policy succeeded only in reducing our defenses to an almost impotent degree and the RAF suffered particularly severely. Despite irrefutable intelligence concerning powerful German arms build-up, various governments chose to seek political gain from pacifist overtures thereby ignoring the urgent defence requirements of the nation. Only in 1936 did the politicians wake up to the threat that Hitler and his legions posed to the peace of Europe and by then it was almost too late.

Panicked into a crash rearmament programme, the government strove to make amends for its previous culpable policies. Expansion of the forces proceeded apace and the RAF urgently wanted pilots.

My father sensed the political climate accurately and pronounced that, 'It was about time that we gave the Hun a kick in the slats again.' My schooldays were almost over at De La Salle College where I strove for good examination marks required for entry into the RAF. These achieved, I applied and was accepted for a short-service commission, but such was the backlog in pilot training I had to wait six months before being called to the flying school.

Contrary to the prevalent public image, military aviation is not just carefree swooping through the clouds. It's a dirty old professional art which becomes more so as the years roll by. As in any profession expertise is gained by experience but, unlike most, a serious incident can be fatally unforgiving and lessons had better be quickly learned if one expects a second chance.

One sunny peacetime day, a few months before World War II broke out, I was detailed as an innocent rookie Spitfire pilot to carry out my first battle climb. This sortie consisted of a climb to the aircraft's ceiling with a full war load of ammunition where the handling characteristics in the rare air could be experienced.

I saw the altimeter slide through 30,000-feet and then I passed out. There was no warning, no sensation – just out like a light. I came to with eyeballs unfocused, dimly seeing a mass of madly spinning dials on the instrument panel, and beyond, through the windscreen, the green and brown outline of the earth. The pain in my ears was excruciating and all I wanted to do was tear my helmet off in a vain effort to relieve the agony. But as my senses and flying instinct rapidly returned, I focussed on the speedily unfolding altimeter and registered a height somewhere in excess of 11,000-feet. Moments later I realised that the clarity with which I could see the trees on the ground meant that I was somewhere below 1,000-feet. I yanked back on the pole, greyed out somewhat and hurtled back to the safety of altitude around 8,000-feet. Misreading the altimeters in use at that period was easy to do and often happened. These instruments were designed on a clock-face principle and in moments of stress it was easy to misread the position of the little hand, which corresponded to the hour hand on a clock, by an error of ten thousand feet.

Having regained a normal flying position I started to sort myself out. My ears still hurt like hell and I developed a sickening headache. My hands and feet were frozen from the low temperatures and I shook all over, not only from the cold but the realisation of the narrow squeak I'd had. As I looked around I found that the oxygen tube from the aircraft supply to my mask had come adrift. In those days the tube hose slid onto a corrugated projection on the side of the facemask and was held in place by the tension of the rubber. Later on the system was modified to a bayonet fitting which couldn't come apart. After this episode I was chary of oxygen systems for the rest of my flying career. Later in the war I was distressed to witness two other aircraft, whose pilots were obviously starved of oxygen, going out of control. Neither recovered before augering in.

I'd been very lucky that I hadn't hit the deck. I hadn't even suffered punctured eardrums which could happen in violent descents from altitude. Luck can contribute to experience and from then on I never took off without constant repeat checks of the oxygen system.

CHAPTER TWO

'PREPARE FOR WAR'

'QUI DESIDERAT PACEM, PRAEPARET BELLUM'
(Let him who desires peace, prepare for war)
Vegetius, 4th Century AD

The amount of flying time which pilots achieve during a career varies considerably. Some exceed 30,000-hours and retire with pulverised backsides and others like myself scrape up around 5,000. But to isolate any particular flight which contributed to those attainments, it's an odds-on bet that the one flight each will remember most clearly will be that of their first solo. In my case I still vividly recall the exhilaration and sense of achievement in poling a Blackburn B2 around the Brough circuit with an empty seat beside me lately occupied by my trusting instructor George Morris.

One Saturday morning in March 1938, we flogged around for half an hour in a series of circuits and bumps at the end of which without any prior warning George taxied into the wind, undid his straps and climbed out of the cockpit. As he leant back in to tidy up the harness he said I could go solo and the exercise was to be just as we had been practising – a circuit and hopefully a safe arrival back to pick him up.

Things went nearly to plan. A more or less straight take-off and climb out over the River Humber, a left-hand turn at a thousand feet above the cement works and on to the downwind leg. Cockpit check for engine revs, airspeed, oil temp and pressure. Then with the sight of the Blackburn aircraft factory emerging from under the lower port wing tip, to enter the final descent and approach. This was the moment of truth as I steered G-ACLD on to a heading which gave a sporting chance of avoiding contact with the factory buildings, When I throttled back, the old crate sank down and shed height as I struggled to hold the airspeed within 20-mph either way of the recommended glide speed. Everything seemed fine and all set for touch down as I floated over the airfield boundary about 400-feet too high. The truth dawned - I'd cocked it up, and my telepathy zeroed in on George Morris's fervent prayer as it floated heavenwards past me, so I gunned the throttle for an overshoot. Having again set up the downwind leg I turned on to the descent behind the factory, but this time with the approach speed more within limits. The touchdown off the third bounce was faultless and I taxied back to collect the relieved Morris.

So my first solo was successfully accomplished; the first big step in flying training. It did not seem only six days since I reported to No 4 E & RFTS (Elementary and Reserve Flying Training School) to learn to fly as a prerequisite to a commission in the RAF. When our course assembled that week, we pupil pilots had contributed to a five bob kitty for retention by the first of us to fly solo. This being noon on Saturday we repaired to the clubhouse, collected our first week's pay, and for myself the kitty. We then opened the bar and the first rounds of beer made a noticeable dent in my kitty but it was well worth it. My total dual instruction time that week amounted to 4-hours 15-minutes before soloing, and somewhat elated I shot a telegram off to my father to inform him. Together with his dual time of 1-hour 15-minutes in the RFC, we had both soloed in a total of 5-hours 30-minutes of instruction; which doesn't mean anything except that it boosted our ego.

As training progressed the remaining two months at Brough were increasingly enjoyable as we strove to master the many other aspects of aviation. We practised forced landings, aerobatics, cross-countries and navigation. The ultimate was a successful final proficiency test with a regular RAF flying instructor. When this *ab initio* phase drew to a close; we handed in our flying kit, collected our log books and A licences, and set off on the next step of our training.

This took place at the vast RAF station at Uxbridge composed of innumerable hideous barrack blocks with huge tarmac parade grounds and not an aeroplane in sight. We soon found out why – Bull was the order of every day. While the tailors were busy 'building' our uniforms, we pounded the squares under the merciless eyes of the drill instructors, peppered the pistol range, skewered the sacks with bayonets, paraded for dinner every night, and sat through hours of lectures on King's Regulations, Air Force law, administration and basic medical know-how. The RAF hierarchy decreed that profound knowledge of these ancillary aspects was an essential background to the finished operational pilot. Who were we to disagree when failure in any of the final tests would result in a somewhat premature departure from the Air Force?

After the four-week period nobody was scrubbed, which meant we were either a very bright bunch or more likely that the Air Force was desperate for pilots. We were gazetted as 'Acting Pilot Officers on Probation', emerged from our mess in our brand-new commissioned uniforms, self-consciously returned our first salutes from leering old sweat Erks[1]; in turn flashed our compliments at all line-of-sight figures who sported any gold braid, which at times included some astonished members of the RAF Central Band.

Uxbridge followed Air Council directions to the letter, and before we moved out on our next posting, we were issued certain items of apparel which were considered essential wear by all the best dressed combat pilots. Our armour included webbing, backpack, gas mask, gaiters, tin hat and a fourteen inch bayonet. Bowed down under such impediments, we sallied forth to our next stage of instruction to No 2 Flying Training School at Brize Norton in Oxfordshire.

I then had a setback because study of the flight details showed that I was listed among those earmarked for bomber training, and I had set my sights on being a fighter pilot as my father had been in the past. Fortunately for

[1] 'Erk: RAF slang for airman below the rank of Corporal.

me, a few adjustments were made to the allocations, and the Chief Flying Instructor, Squadron Leader 'Jackie' Horner, switched cockpits for John Barraclough and me. We both had above average ratings at civil flying training school and went our separate ways, he on multi-engines and myself on singles. We were two of the very few on our course who survived the six years of World War II. I have often reflected on what would have happened had not the exchange been made at the time and whether our luck would have held. Paradoxically John embarked on a superb career winding up as a knighted four star Air Chief Marshal, and I as a no star Group Captain. As John wryly remarked, 'It might have been more interesting if one or other of us had not survived!' A few days after the change, I began to wonder whether I'd done the right thing. My flying training was now to be continued on the Hawker Hart, an open two seat biplane, and my instructor was a tough flight lieutenant called Wizzy King. He was the antithesis of the quiet encouraging George Morris at Brough. In his time Wizzy had been an RAF boxing champion, and he tackled the art of flight instruction as though it was a challenge in the ring. Instructions were bellowed down the Gosport tube inter-cockpit communication, and whether or not they were understood by me, he was extremely impatient if I did not react instantly. Often I would just have taken the initial action to execute a manoeuvre and the controls would be wrenched out of my hands with the remark, 'Not that way, you bloody fool'.

I felt quite unsettled by this treatment and after this first dual trip in the Hart was even more discouraged as we taxied in when he wanted to know who the hell gave me the idea that I thought I could fly. After a few careful inquiries, I discovered that this was Wizzy's normal method of instruction and that he was running true to type. I resolved there and then that I would stick it out which I managed to do to keep up with the programme, but once or twice I thought he was going to win the battle. An instance I recall was my first instruction in spin recovery on instruments. My pre-flight briefing for this was a bit shattering:

'Oxspring, have you ever been air sick?'

'No, sir.'

'Well, get in the back seat of that Hart, you damn soon will be.'

We tried hard. Shut in the cockpit, enclosed by a green canvas hood, I had no view other than the inside of the cockpit. With each spin the instruments gyrated crazily and each time my senses whirled round in a dizzy vertigo, a nauseous sensation intensified by a repulsive smell from the radiator. In practice spins it was a usual procedure to retract the radiator in order to keep up the engine temperature. This configuration led to a flow of obnoxious fumes from a mixture of hot oil and coolant, normally dispersed in the slipstream, pulsing back through the inside of the fuselage. Normally these gases escaped through the open cockpits, but with the blind flying canopy in place some were trapped in the rear to the discomfiture of the unfortunate occupant. After a dozen or so consecutive spins alternating to left and right, I still hung on to my breakfast but was almost past caring. Fortunately spin recovery is a fairly simple procedure and the last few I executed almost automatically. Perhaps Wizzy, in his open front cockpit where he could see everything, was beginning to feel as sick as I did. I hoped so, and was very relieved when he called a halt and let me pull back the canopy and breathe some fresh air. My digestive juices were still intact and I believed I'd won this psychological round. Moreover, after this experience I knew I was never likely to be sick in the air and this subsequently proved to be true.

The next big round in the contest with Wizzy involved my initiation into the art of night flying. After a typically crisp briefing in which I was told there was nothing more to flying by night than by day except that it was dark, we took to the air. The first circuit was a demonstration approach and landing, and I had a brief chance to look around. Brize Norton looked completely different by night, mostly fathomless black depths dispersed by little pinpricks of lights. I could see the flare-path all right, and that at any rate was the main thing as far as this flight was concerned.

Wizzy brought the Hart round the pattern and headed downward toward the flare path. As we passed the Chance light, a large floodlight illuminating the initial part of the flare path, I saw the ground for the first time. Apparently Wizzy didn't. Without any flare out or gentle float before touch-down, the Hart rammed its wheels into the grass with a teeth-jarring bump causing us to bound into the air again in a gigantic kangaroo hop. Fascinated I watched the flarepath recede for long moments and then rush to meet us once more. Again we struck the ground with a clout which must have strained the Oleos to their limits. Once more we bounced into the air. This time Wizzy caught it with full throttle and we climbed away into the night to set up another attack on the landing strip.

We got back to circuit height where Wizzy told me to hold the controls and follow him through another landing. I seriously doubted that I would be able to emulate the previous demonstration but I did as I was told. We contacted the ground again in much the same manner as before and I had to admire the consistency. This time, however, it was accompanied by a verbal blast from Wizzy demanding how the hell could he demonstrate night landings if my ham hands prevented him from moving the controls properly.

After an hour's repeat performances in which we continued to arrive on the flarepath in a series of semi-controlled crashes, each one accompanied by blistering comments from the back seat, we gave up and taxied in. Other pupils were night soloing after about an hour's dual and it would have been a black mark against both of us if I failed. As the Hart stopped on the flight line, Wizzy surprised me by asking me if I thought I could go solo. I felt I could hardly do worse and assented at once. I carried out two solo circuits and landings, and from then on I was much more confident.

After this, there was a mutual air of 'no contest' between Wizzy and I, and the intermediate flying stage was harmoniously concluded in three intensive months. After passing written examinations in all the related ground subjects, we paraded in front of the Air Officer Commanding in Chief to receive our wings.

This all occurred during the period of the Munich crisis when the country was at panic stations over the possibility of war with Germany. At the same time at Brize, a memorable occasion took place in the form of a demonstration of performance by three of our latest fighters under development. These were the Hurricane, Spitfire and the Martin Baker. The Brass flew in from all directions to witness the displays flown by the respective test pilots.

The Hurricane and Spitfire performed in the manner which is so well-known, and the Martin Baker appeared to equal its now illustrious sisters. Compared with the other two, it looked rather primitive but like them it was a monoplane with an enclosed cockpit, carried eight machine-guns, and was similarly powered by a Rolls Royce engine. At low altitude, its manoeuvrability was impressive, even though unlike the others it had a fixed undercarriage with the wheels enclosed in streamlined cowls which made it appear the ugly sister of the trio. It was rejected for production for the Air Force probably on the grounds of cost and a slightly inferior performance, but whatever the reasons, to me in hindsight, it was a great pity it was never accepted. It was certainly greatly superior in performance to other ageing fighters of the time such as the Gauntlet, the Gladiator and the Fury. What a difference it would have made in 1940 if we'd had an additional twenty-five squadrons of Martin Baker fighters to get stuck into the *Luftwaffe*.

We now entered the advanced training phase where our instruction was geared to operational roles of the squadrons to which we would be posted. Half a dozen of us went to the fighter flight equipped with Hawker Furies. The Fury was a super little single seat open cockpit biplane of the Hart family which had been in squadron service since 1932, but which by now was obsolete for front line service. It was a delightful aircraft to fly being light and responsive on all controls. Our mentor and flight commander, Steve Godden, was a dyed in the wool fighter pilot. He weaved us through all the fighter gambits with verve and elan; advanced instruction, use of the Aldis sight, standard attacks using camera and live ammunition, and generally punching home the basics required for fighter combat. He and his staff took each of us up in the dual instruction Hart and put us through advanced aerobatics involving vertical rolls, flick rolls, Immelmanns and bunts.

Gradually our confidence and ability increased, and finally we went down to Warmwell in Dorset to try our expertise on the firing ranges at Chesil Bank. The Fury was an ideal chariot for these exercises, being operated in the fighter environment for which it was designed. We were now beginning to feel part of the aircraft, moving as it were into each manoeuvre as one entity and not just being taken along for the ride.

The Fury was armed with twin Vickers machine-guns mounted along the top fuselage in front of the pilot and synchronized to fire through the propeller arc. The belt feeds and breeches were located under the top cockpit cowling and consequently were within reach of the pilot. The armament practices produced their challenges because the guns had tendencies to jam during the firing, and when this happened we were expected to use our classroom teaching to clear the stoppages in flight before continuing. Sometimes this necessitated the change of breech block which could only be achieved with gloveless hands. This was easier to do in the classroom than in the draughty cockpit of a lively little fighter which had to be flown at the same time. Many were the gashed and bloody fingers which returned to base from these flights. Be that as it may, we had fun and learned a lot.

We flew back to Brize where we were notified of our squadron postings. We had a cracking farewell guest night which my father attended, and next day trundled off to our new stations. To my great delight, my destination was No 66 Squadron at Duxford in Cambridgeshire, one of the first two squadrons to be equipped with the Spitfire.

CHAPTER THREE

'KEEP IT ON THE AIRFIELD'

Flight Lieutenant Jimmy Jago

It was just before Christmas when I checked in to my new outfit. The squadron was in the final stages of re-equipment of its aircraft from Gloster Gauntlets to Supermarine Spitfires. 66 was the second unit in the Air Force to be armed with Spits as No 19 which was also at Duxford had already filled its complement. Our hangar was full of aircraft. The Gauntlets were being made ready for disposal, and at the same time the ground crews were being trained in all the servicing and maintenance required for the Spitfire. Much to my disappointment I never got a ride in a Gauntlet since the flight commander didn't want to risk any unserviceability before the biplanes left.

The weather during the following months was bad and very little flying took place. But I was kept gainfully occupied in getting to know the vital engine and armament systems of the Spitfire with occasional flights in the squadron Magister in order to get familiar with the local area.

On 2nd February, 1939, the great day came. I strapped into Spitfire K9802 for my first solo hour of what was ultimately to total 1,488-hours in most marks of Spit up to the 22. I taxied gingerly across the airfield to take-off point and turned into wind. Opening up the power gently to avoid a violent swing which would otherwise ensue, I started the take-off run. As briefed I held the stick central to prevent the tail coming too far up. This could easily happen with the powerful elevator controls where it was only too easy to catch the large two bladed fixed pitch prop on the ground. The rest of the take-off was easy, and as the aircraft assumed its natural flight attitude the nose lowered and forward visibility improved considerably. The next action was one unique to early Spitfires which entailed getting the undercarriage retracted before the airspeed built up too high. This was a manual action whereby the pilot had to lock the throttle in climb power with his left hand, transfer this hand to the control column, at the same time moving his right hand to an undercarriage retraction pump handle – and start pumping. It took time until pilots new to the aircraft got used to these procedures. The energetic pumping motion of the right hand inevitably resulted in an alternate reaction with the left hand which was guiding the aircraft, and this sequence in turn resulted in the most extraordinary flight gyrations on the climb out. Sometimes on formation take-offs it got really hairy, especially at night. After some experience most pilots managed to control it. My method was to dig my left elbow into my groin and hold the stick level with fingers and thumb until the wheels locked up.

Many pilots have written of their thrills, exhilaration and delight on their first solos in a Spitfire. I will not enlarge on that except to say that I agree with them, and to emphasise the confidence we had in the instant response of power in the growling Rolls Royce Merlin II engines. After being airborne for nearly an hour getting the feel of the Spit with power on, power off, in climb descent and turn, I returned to the circuit, pumped the gear down and settled down on Duxford's expansive grass airfield.

From then on the training intensity built up. With the spring, the weather improved and we flew almost daily. Formation cross-countries, battle climbs to altitude, fighter attack practice, night flying, aerobatics and all the other exercises designed to produce an effective fighter pilot. I was still the bog rat of the squadron, but all my seniors relentlessly drilled their skills into me. The cross section of pilots of the squadron reflected the principle which Lord Trenchard had stressed since RFC days; that it was not the

British Air Force, but the *Royal* Air Force and as such was comprised of the cream of aircrew from all the Commonwealth countries. 66 Squadron's CO was Squadron Leader J D Fuller-Good (an old sweat from the North-West Frontier), Flight Commander Jimmy Jago (British), Dicky Power (Australian), Jack Grafstra (Canadian), Zulu Heath (South African), Lobber Hyde (New Zealander), and the rest from all parts of the UK.

Training to be a fighter pilot, though always exhilarating and every flight a challenge, sometimes provided occasions above the norm. Such was the case on the squadron's second night flying programme in April '39. At that period the aids to achieving successful sorties in the dark were primitive to say the least. There were no illuminated runways with approach and boundary lights, merely a single line flarepath of goose neck paraffin flares laid in a straight line across the grass airfield. The only other assistance was a diesel generated flood light giving a flat illumination along the first two hundred yards of the landing area.

I sped along the flarepath in the wake of four others. Three of them were practising night formation and the fourth chap and myself were on sector reconnaissance. It was a beautiful night, full brilliant moon, stars, perfect visibility, and all the street-lit towns standing out in clusters. Several others had taken off after me and altogether there were nine aircraft up.

I could see the massive glow of light from London and the various flashing red beacons identifying the RAF aerodromes in East Anglia, one of which was my own base at Duxford. I was about thirty miles from home at the end of the recce when the friendly morse coded 'DX' of Duxford's beacon disappeared, and in spite of straining my eyes I could not see it any more. I flew on the course back and found myself over Royston, not more than seven miles from base. I was then somewhat concerned to see that a layer of low stratus cloud had formed beneath me and stretched north as far as I could see. Jimmy Jago, the flight commander, had just landed with his formation and gave a radio call instructing all those of us still airborne to land immediately. I flew over the top of the stratus which was at 1,000-feet and the base, Jimmy said, was 200-feet. He despatched indicator rockets up through the clouds to indicate the position of the airfield beneath. After the second rocket I saw Pat Browne's formation of three and an odd aircraft which I knew to be that of Duggie Paton.

I was instructed to come down and land, so I gently sank through the stratus from on top at 1,000-feet and broke out of cloud about 200-feet over a local village. I called for more rockets and one was fired which steered me to the circuit. Just then I heard the boys still circling above being ordered to divert to Debden.

As I orbited Duxford at the uncomfortable height of 200-feet there seemed to be precious little light on the airfield. I later found that Sergeant Ward who had landed a few minutes ahead of me had hit the flood light on touch-down, and had written off both it and his aircraft but was unhurt.

I put down the wheel and flaps and made a long, low, flat approach. Anxious not to stall, I came in too fast and eventually touched down halfway along the flarepath going like a bat out of hell. I knew it would be a bit dodgy in those conditions to try and overshoot with the fixed pitch wooden prop and I didn't much want to either. Consequently, I ruddered my direction towards the far corner of the grass field, crossed the flarepath, and headed through the blackness toward the boundary fence which I saw looming up. I braced myself and waited for the inevitable awful things to happen. But they didn't. There was first a bump like a bad landing, and the aircraft came to rest still the right way up. I turned off the fuel cock, ran the carburettor dry, and switched off magnetos and nav lights. Clambering out, I realised that I had gone through a hedge, over the Royston to Newmarket road, bounced over a ditch, through another hedge and into a muddy field behind the officers' married quarters. Meanwhile, consternation reigned on the other side of the road. Fire tender and blood wagon were chasing up and down the road accompanied by Jimmy Jago on his bicycle. Nothing could be actually seen in the dark because the aircraft wheels had left no sign of their passing through the brush fence. Eventually my position was located, and with a number of ground troops and pilots we manhandled the Spit back along the main road to the guardroom which was the only way back to the hangars. The total damage turned out to be two dents in the under-carriage fairings and some hedge twigs in the radiator, but Jimmy Jago was not impressed. 'Next time you bring one in', he said, 'keep it on the airfield'.

The summer of '39 sped by as the political tension mounted and we intensified our fighter training. It wasn't without penalty though. One night we lost Duggie Paton who crashed into a small hill just east of Duxford, having been caught in much the same circumstances as I had that night in April.

In August, war was imminent, and the squadrons at Duxford were moved out to dispersal points around the field and away from the hangars. On 3rd September all squadrons were at readiness and we had just heard on the radio Mr Chamberlain's declaration of war on Germany, when operations rang through and scrambled one aircraft. I was the one despatched and on getting airborne was told I was to try and intercept and destroy a barrage balloon which had broken loose at Liverpool, and was last reported in the Huntingdon area about 10,000-feet. Had an interception been made it could have been likely that my Spitfire's guns would have been the first to fire in World War II; albeit on such an unlikely target. But tracking down that balloon was like looking for a needle in a haystack. I never found it and so returned to base.

There was an air of hypertension among all ranks of Fighter Command as we awaited the expected German bomber onslaught, and early on 6th September the over anxiousness of the air defence network led to the historic incident to be known in perpetuity as 'The Battle of Barking Creek'. Searchlight crews on the coast south of Colchester reported an approaching raid of German aircraft and the information duly appeared on the 11 Group plotting tables. Trigger happy anti-aircraft gun crews opened up in the Thames estuary on imaginary targets, and this spurred the 11 Group controller at Uxbridge to scramble squadrons from North Weald and Hornchurch to investigate the activity along the Essex coast.

As the confusion mounted, touchy controllers of adjoining sectors, anxious not to be caught with their pants down, despatched more fighters from their bases. The controller at Debden who was becoming increasingly concerned at the mounting aerial frenzy so near to his area told his 'Ops B' assistant to scramble a 'section'. Ops B, a Reserve pilot officer who had been in uniform for all of three days, enthusiastically complied and cranked the phone through to the duty Hurricane squadron. Unfortunately he got his terminology mixed and ordered a 'squadron' scramble. Instead of three aircraft getting airborne from Debden the controller was blissfully unaware that twelve Hurricanes had hurtled aloft and were headed east toward the escalating activity.

Just to complicate the issue, the border separating the adjoining 11 and 12 Groups ran between Debden and Duxford, which were only ten miles apart. At 12 Group headquarters miles away near Nottingham the duty controller was becoming highly agitated at the inexplicable panic so close to his southern boundary. His reaction was predictable in that to ensure being on the safe side he scrambled both 19 and 66 Squadrons from Duxford. These two outfits had their Spitfires dispersed along opposite sides of the airfield and unfortunately neither knew that the other had been ordered off.

There being little wind, each unit's fighters took off straight ahead towards each other. I was on the left flank of B Flight 66 Squadron and managed to bank left away from the onrushing 19 Squadron. Twenty-four Spitfires miraculously managed to dodge each other employing wildly unorthodox manoeuvres which resulted in a cloud of milling aircraft over Duxford. Pilots were inexorably split from their basic formations and in trying to sort out the shambles, looked desperately around for their leaders. I had taken off as Green 3 in 66 Squadron and wound up leading the remains of Red section in 19 Squadron. After some minutes of chaos, the two shaken squadron commanders managed to get the message through for everyone to land.

Meanwhile the Hornchurch Spitfires intercepted the North Weald Hurricanes and, since aircraft recognition was not among the strong points of the day, a hectic dog fight ensued in which two Hurricanes were shot down. So ended 'The Battle of Barking Creek' on the fourth day of the war. At least it exposed glaring deficiencies in aircraft identification and control procedures. In a hard way it was a blessing in disguise, and much was achieved during the ensuing months to rectify the problems. On the other hand, there was no doubt that we fighter pilots were on our toes and raring to go. If the redoubtable *Luftwaffe* bombers were reluctant to launch their expected offensive on the UK defenses, Fighter Command's squadrons showed no compunction in sustaining the mounting tension by knocking the hell out of each other.

Fighter Command was rapidly forming more squadrons, as a result trained pilots were being shifted around. Jimmy Jago was posted for weapons training at Manby. It shattered us to hear shortly afterwards that he had been killed in a Fury when he hit a ground target as he pulled out of an attack. Tim Craxton was posted to what was to become the Photographic Reconnaissance Unit, flying Spitfires with special cameras. The CO, Fuller-Goode, had gone and his place was taken by Squadron Leader E George. Razz Berry was commissioned from Sergeant to Pilot Officer and posted. He was to go on to survive the war as the most successful fighter pilot to emerge from 66, credited with seventeen aircraft destroyed. Zulu Heath went to Bomber Command only to be killed later over Norway in a Blenheim. Dicky Power was transferred to 504 City of Nottingham Auxiliary Squadron flying Hurricanes.

We faced the freezing winter of 39/40. Since this was part of the phoney war, the *Luftwaffe* generated very little action. We spent most of the time in cold unheated dispersals at Watton and Horsham interrupted by twice daily convoy patrols over the North Sea. For some reason ops always wanted these patrols flown at heights between 25,000 and 30,000-feet. We seemed to spend the entire winter in fleece-lined jackets, trousers and flying boots and never getting warm. As we clambered up to high altitudes the unpressurised cockpit sucked in icy draughts from the intensely cold atmosphere. Hands and feet, already cold before take-off, got steadily more numb. Once at altitude, we settled down to an hour's freezing patrol up and down a twenty mile-long beat over the east coast convoys. Everything went Arctic. Mist formed on the glass of the instruments and hoar frost covered the inside of the canopy, which got worse as the moisture from our breath froze on oxygen masks. Occasionally we suffered from the dreaded 'bends'. The reduced atmospheric pressure caused the muscles to swell inducing lactic acid particularly in the elbow, knee and ankle joints. It caused a painful and persistent ache, and once smitten the pain could only be abated by a descent to lower altitude. If the ops controller refused requests to reduce height when the bends set in, we'd have to sweat it out for the remainder of the patrol.

On the let-down at the end of the patrol, we would point our aircraft out to sea and press the firing button just to see how many guns were so frozen up they wouldn't fire. Usually a couple would not. The monitoring of these shipping patrols was pleasantly interrupted around Christmas time when we had to escort the cruiser HMS *Ajax* as she returned from the naval battle of the River Plate. She looked magnificent in her tropical warpaint, steaming north at over 20 knots for her well-earned refit after participating in the battle that led to the scuttling of the *Graf Spee*.

After a jaunt to Cambridge one evening we returned to the mess at Duxford. Sitting in the ante room was a solitary figure wearing a Flying Officer's stripe on his uniform. For this rank he seemed a little older than most of us and our new squadron leader, Rupert Leigh, greeted him enthusiastically. They had been at Cranwell together a decade before and Rupert introduced us. Slowly the story unfolded. We were chatting with Douglas Bader who had lost his legs in a flying accident in 1931, and had somehow persuaded the Air Ministry to accept him back in the RAF. He moved on his artificial legs almost as actively as any of us. We were vastly impressed, and even more so the next day when he Joined his flight in 19 Squadron. Flying a Spitfire for the first time he finished the flight with an impeccable display of acrobatics before pulling off a perfect landing. His dynamic personality inspired confidence, and no one was surprised when his subsequent heroic exploits made him a legend in his time.

Another superlative character to grace the Duxford portals was Squadron Leader (later Group Captain) A B Woodhall MC. An ex-Royal Flying Corps pilot, Woody had known my father in 54 Squadron during World War I. In 1940 he built up the Duxford Sector operations room and became the RAF's most celebrated fighter controller. His feel for an intercept, providing his fighters with the most advantageous positionings, was uncanny. In sector operations at Duxford, followed by command of the Tangmere sector and ultimately as operations controller in the crucial siege of Malta, his fame spread throughout the fighter world. Wearing his indispensable monocle he was easily recognised, and his squeeze box accordion accompaniments to bawdy songs in off duty moments were memories to cherish.

The phoney war dragged on until on 9th April the balloon went up when Hitler invaded Denmark and Norway. A hastily assembled British Expeditionary Force was despatched to Namsos in the vain hope of denying Trondheim and northern Norway to the German advance. The wing included No 263 Fighter Squadron equipped with Gladiators capable of operating from naval aircraft carriers. The only possible base from which the squadron could function was a highly unsuitable frozen lake for which it was almost impossible to provide adequate ground support equipment. The outcome was predictable, and although the Glads managed to fly off the carrier *Glorious* to the lake, the *Luftwaffe* was waiting for them. Having no radar warning, no starter batteries, no oxygen and fuel only available in four gallon tins, the odds were stacked against them. Ten Gladiators were written off in the first *Luftwaffe* attack on the lake. Somehow four fighters managed to crank up their engines on internal batteries and get airborne. During the day these four managed to account for five of their attackers but the whole gallant episode was a lost cause. At the end of the day, with no aircraft left serviceable, 263 Squadron's pilots were evacuated aboard the carrier *Furious* and returned to Scotland.

The army troops of the British Expeditionary Force were still in Norway and hopes were still alive that Narvik could be recaptured and defended. 263 Squadron reformed at Turnhouse with new Gladiators but needed reinforcing with more pilots. Consequently a number of fully trained pilots were posted in from other squadrons in Fighter Command. I was the one that 66 Squadron had to cough up and at lunchtime on 8th May my posting came through, giving me about two hours to clear the station and catch the night train to Edinburgh.

I got to Turnhouse the next morning to find the airfield a hive of activity. 263 Squadron had been joined by 46 Hurricane Squadron and preparations were well advanced for early embarkation in the carrier *Furious*. About half a dozen of us newly-posted pilots had never flown a Gladiator before, and great efforts were being made to get each of us airborne on at least one familiarisation trip. My turn to fly the Glad came in the late evening and I strapped in and taxied out. I got to the downwind end of the airfield and faced round for take-off. Instead of getting the green light to go ahead, I got a red light which aborted the trip. I taxied back to the flight line where my flight commander, R S Mills, informed me that he had decided it was too late for me to fly that evening, and that I was to go next morning. A heavy beer session ensued for the rest of the evening and finally we fell into bed.

First thing next morning, orders came through for 263 to fly on to *Furious* where 46 Squadron's Hurricanes were already on board. The squadron took off and landed on *Furious* which was steaming down the Forth. This left four of us replacement pilots who had not yet flown the Glad standing around at Turnhouse. Just before he took off, I asked Mills what we were to do. He just said for us catch a resupply ship and join the rest in Norway.

We hung around Turnhouse for nearly a week but it was all too obvious that no more ships were due to sail and I finally phoned my old squadron and told the CO, Rupert Leigh, of my predicament. He got cracking and next day orders arrived reposting me back to 66. I lost no time in getting a train down south and reporting back to the squadron which since I left had moved to Horsham St Faith.

In the meantime, 263 and 46 Squadrons got to Norway where they were in hectic action for over two weeks before the final evacuation of the country was ordered. The two squadrons flew on to the carrier *Glorious* for the withdrawal back to the UK. Unfortunately, the return voyage was intercepted by the formidable German battleships *Scharnhorst* and *Gneisenau*. Under heavy gunfire, the *Glorious* sank blazing from bow to stern. With her went all the fine pilots of 263 and 46 Squadrons. Only two survived, Bing Cross and Jamie Jamieson, who somehow managed to climb on a survival float and endured five days and nights of bitter cold in the North Sea before being rescued.

Fortune certainly smiled on me that evening of 9th May when I never got airborne in the Glad. Had I done so the chances are that I would have gone down with all the others in the *Glorious*.

During the ten days I had been away, 66 Squadron had not been idle. On 10th May the surging attack of the German *blitzkreig* had blasted through the Ardennes and Maastricht and had flooded through the Low Countries towards France. In three days the River Meuse was crossed, and in a further two the Panzers were through the key defence point at the Sedan gap. As the German army maintained its momentum into North-East France, the Allies were forced to retreat with the British and Belgian armies backing on the Channel coast as the French retreated towards Paris.

Daily the situation got more desperate and the calls for RAF fighter support more urgent. Fighter Command was already weakened by the deployment of ten Hurricane squadrons to France which were already being decimated by overwhelming numbers of *Luftwaffe* fighters. Head of Fighter Command, Sir Hugh Dowding, pleaded with the War Cabinet not to reduce his strength of squadrons further since due to its depleted strength, the air defence of Britain was already at risk. Winston Churchill, who had just taken the helm as Prime Minister, agreed with the C-in-C and the decision was made not to despatch any more of Fighter Command's precious squadrons to France. However, the British Expeditionary Force urgently required support for its withdrawal along the French coast. Consequently, a large number of our home-based units were deployed forward on Manston and Hawkinge. Controlled to some extent by 11 Group they attempted to ward off the constant *Luftwaffe* dive bombing which was harassing our soldiers.

Sixty-six Squadron played their part in this, but due to the lack of adequate radar coverage from England the interceptions were very much a hit and miss affair. Nevertheless the air activity was so intense that contact with the *Luftwaffe* was inevitable, and a series of non-conclusive combats ensued. No positive claims were made by the squadron but a couple of the pilots were shot up and had to crash land after one of the skirmishes.

I rejoined the squadron on 19th May and my twenty-first birthday on the 22nd coincided with the initial move in the withdrawal from Dunkirk. By 1st June the evacuation of the troops by the Navy and the little ships was fully under way covered by the hard-worked fighter squadrons of 11 Group. At the same time reinforcement was provided by 12 Group squadrons concentrated forward on Martlesham Heath. We in 66 were among them, but to my chagrin I did not get a ride until the last day. Although now a full blown Pilot Officer I was still the senior bog rat and my position was similar to being primary substitute in a football team. The first team flew all the sorties until on that final day one member had engine trouble before take-off and I joined up with the reserve aircraft.

On that bright summer day, navigation to Dunkirk was no problem. A great pall of smoke, which we could clearly see from Martlesham some 65 miles distant, arose from the fires at the stricken port of burning buildings, vehicles, vessels, fuel dumps and anything which would ignite. All kinds of ships, yachts, boats and almost anything that would float was strung out across the Channel from the Dunkirk beaches to North and South

Foreland.

We swept inland of the smoke at about 15,000-feet looking for the *Luftwaffe*, but what we encountered were either already engaged by other fighter squadrons, or too far away to chase without burning off our limited fuel. So rather disappointed at not having a chance to get stuck in, we completed our patrol and returned to base. There was no further opportunity to operate as that evening the epic evacuation was completed. The vast majority of our gallant expeditionary force had come home.

Returning to 12 Group, we opened up a brand-new base at Coltishall. As the dust of Dunkirk settled we reverted to the boring convoy patrols off the East Anglia coast. The *Luftwaffe* had gone to ground for a while, no doubt to build up its strength for the assault on England.

One day in early July, we had a VIP visitor. The Prime Minister, Winston Churchill stumped around our dispersal points and had a chat with us all. He asked how things were going and the main complaint to him was the lack of activity which, apart from Dunkirk, we had borne for nearly a year. His response to us was to be patient because very soon we would have as much as we wanted. A few days later he made his famous speech to the nation about the defence of our islands.

'The Battle of France is over, the Battle for Britain is about to begin.'

How right he was!

CHAPTER FOUR

'We Shall Never Surrender'

Winston Churchill

Within a couple of weeks of Mr Churchill's visit, the game was on. Hitler's planned invasion of Britain, code-named '*Sealion*', was intended to be launched in mid-September. But no such step could be taken until the *Luftwaffe* had gained air supremacy over the Channel and Southern England.

At the same time, the C-in-C Fighter Command's urgent priority was to build up his fighter strength. New squadrons were being formed as fast as resources would permit. In consequence, it was necessary to milk the regular force of fully trained pilots in order to provide experience and leadership in the new units. 66 suffered its share in losing a hard core of 'old-timers' who were promoted to become flight commanders. Frankie Rimmer, Bill Smith and George Brown moved to Hurricane squadrons, Jerry Jones and Hugh Kennard to other Spitfire outfits. Jack Grafstra and Ed Campbell-Colquhoun shifted to the newly formed Defiant night fighters. We missed these chaps a great deal but there was no staying their deserved promotions and those of us remaining had to knuckle down and give their highly promising replacements some intensive training. Among the latter were Pickering, Bodie and Kendal, all of whom were later to fight with commendable dash and guts, only to lose their lives the following year.

Despite the German presence on the French side of the Channel, the Royal Navy was still escorting convoys of ships with vital supplies for our southern ports. In early July the *Luftwaffe* exploded into ferocious dive bombing attacks against our Channel shipping. As intended these attacks provoked Fighter Command into action to defend the ships and fierce engagements ensued. The swarms of Messerschmitt fighters in greatly superior numbers set about their task of smashing the resistance of the RAF squadrons. Fortunately, the German intentions foundered on their miscalculation of the effectiveness of the British early warning and fighter control network, together with the resultant savage reaction of the RAF fighter squadrons. Being able to concentrate his resistance to the enemy air onslaught, the Commander-in-Chief, Sir Hugh Dowding, was therefore able to husband his precious reserves. Effectively, the few squadrons in the south of England shouldered the fighting, and after three weeks of constant action, pilots were near exhaustion.

In spite of the daily bitter actions over our shipping, the strength of the RAF resistance did not diminish and the German attacks then switched to our fighter airfields where it hurt most. This was the most telling tactic used so far, and had it been continued for a longer period than in fact was the case, Fighter Command's resistance would have been annihilated.

Hornchurch, Kenley, Biggin Hill, North Weald, Northolt, Tangmere, Croydon, Middle Wallop, Duxford and Debden all suffered devastating attacks. Many of our fighters caught on the ground endeavouring to rearm and refuel were either destroyed or severely damaged. In some cases, the operations rooms, which were unfortunately located on the airfields, were written off. Manston, Hawkinge, Lympne, Detling and Eastchurch were plastered so hard that their operational units were withdrawn.

Whilst the squadrons of 11 and 10 Groups were battling desperately against massive odds, we in 12 and 13 Groups had to sit out of the action. In compliance with Stuffy Dowding's strategy, we were only to be committed when his southern squadrons needed urgent relief. This was accentuated, as we were to find out, years later, by the extraordinary, reluctance of the AOC 11 Group, Air Vice-Marshal Keith Park, to call for assistance from his opposite number in 12 Group when he was hard-pressed. This all stemmed from a personal antipathy and rivalry between the two commanders which at times had serious consequences. It was frustrating in the extreme to be sitting at Collishall less than 100-miles away from the hectic air fighting raging in the south with little chance of helping out. So, as we impatiently awaited our call to the contest, we carried on with our boring convoy patrols off the east coast.

Suddenly, during one of these sorties off Lowestoft, our morale took an uplift. In the afternoon of 29th July, I was leading Blue Section with Peter Studd and 'Pickles' Pickering when control vectored us on to a Heinkel 111. We sighted it flying at 15,000-feet on a northerly heading a few miles east of the convoy. I put the section into line astern and led the attack in from above. I misjudged the approach and had to close from dead astern to get into range. As we did so, the rear gunner opened fire, his tracers going to my right side and below. Closing in to about 400-yards, I let go with a long burst and then broke up and away to starboard. I didn't see any hits on the Heinkel, but its rear fire had ceased. Peter and Pickle followed in with their attacks and then we scissored the target from the beams. The Heinkel's wheels dropped down as he headed for some stratus cloud around 8,000-feet. We picked him up again underneath the layer and expended the remainder of our ammo into him. He went down with both engines on fire to ditch in the sea. We stayed long enough to see two of the crew clamber out into their dinghy before the aircraft sank from sight. Back home at Coltishall, we stuck in our combat reports claiming our first victim.

The hot summer flowed into August and the ferocity of the air battles south of London intensified. Despite this, our inactivity continued and at the end of the month, not having had any leave for over a year, I took a few days off and went home to Sheffield. The very next day, the squadron received the long awaited call to move south into 11 Group. The following evening I was ordered to rejoin 66 at Kenley and caught the first train for London. When I arrived at Whyteleafe station, there being no transport in sight, I lugged my suitcase up the hill to the officers' mess.

There I was met by a bunch of 66 pilots. They looked a sorry sight, a couple of them sporting bandages and all of them exceedingly scruffy. A flow of facetious remarks greeted me such as, 'What kept you?' and 'Wait till you get a basin of this lot!'

Much had happened in the brief four days I had been away. My flight commander, Billy Burton, had been promoted to squadron commander of No 616 Squadron the day after I went on leave. His place was taken by a posted-in Canadian, Pat Christie, who shot down a Messerschmitt 109 the next day and himself then got clobbered and severely wounded. So I'd already had a new flight commander I'd never even met. Flight Lieutenant F P R Dunworth, Pilot Officers C A Cooke and A N R L Appleford together with Sergeant A D Smith had all stopped their various packets from the busy Messerschmitt 109's. Cooky baled out with painful burns, Dunworth and Apple both crash-landed with wounds and, worst of all, Smudger Smith, one of our most senior pilots, baled out with horrible wounds and burns, only to die in agony the following evening.

On 5th September, as I was travelling back, the 109's were again active. Peter King was killed as he went in with his aircraft, but fortunately Dizzy Allen and Johnny Mather were unhurt as they crash-landed their stricken Spits.

Promotions, postings and casualties had now rocketed me in the space of two months from humble bog rat to senior pilot officer. With Pat Christie *hors de combat*, B flight was minus a flight commander and in consequence it fell to me to fill the vacancy.

The squadron's casualties were alarming. We had lost eight aircraft and six pilots in two days fighting. Dunworth was promoted to take over 54 Squadron and Ken Gillies, who had flown with 66 for over four years, was now A Flight commander. His extensive fighter training and natural flying ability led him to adapt easily to the hectic air combat demands of 1940. He gave me some sound tactical advice as to how to react when I made my baptism in battle the following day. His concluding remark was, 'Whatever circus you get tangled up in, Bobby, for Christ's sake watch your tail!' His words were prophetic.

Shortly after ten o'clock next morning, the squadron was scrambled and vectored to the Maidstone area. We climbed at full bore to around 15,000-feet and as we levelled off, a sighting was called by one of our pilots. *'Fibus Leader bandits eleven o'clock level'*. The rest of us eyeballed the indicated area.

At least one other among us was impressed for a voice transmitted the highly useless comment, 'God, look at 'em, hundreds of the bastards.'

Up front the squadron leader, Rupert Leigh, did not have time to admonish the culprit but merely gave the Tally Ho and ordered us into attack formation. The leading German bomber waves were now on our port side and slightly below. As the CO's six Spits peeled down on to them, we in B flight positioned to follow behind and I noticed a dog fight in progress above and up sun. Four grey-painted Messerschmitt 109's flew close over the top of us, climbing away. As we started to follow the CO, a 109 flashed vertically down in front of my nose. His belly was toward me so close I could distinguish rivets and oil streaks on his fuselage. Flames and black smoke were streaming from his engine as he disappeared beneath me; the vanquished victim of one of our hawk-eyed boys up top in the dog fight.

Still turning toward the bombers, I saw another 109 crossing ahead at my level. I throttled up to max power to reduce the distance and get my sights on. Just getting to firing range, I suddenly thought of Ken's 'watch your tail' warning. I looked back over my left shoulder and sure enough, another 109 was below my tail pulling a bead and about to let go. There was no point sticking around to see if he could shoot straight and my reactions were unbelievably fast. I parked everything in the left-hand corner. Cranking on full left aileron and rudder, at the same time I shoved the throttle through the gate for emergency power.

Hauling back on the stick, I reefed into a blacked-out turn. As I was in the grey-out stage, I noticed I'd got the nose above the horizon, which gave some assurance that, on recovery, I would have gained precious feet in altitude. The blood drained from my eyes as the G forces blacked me out. Sweat ran down my face greasing the chamois-lined oxygen mask which slid a couple of inches down my nose.

I held the turn for a number of seconds which from experience I judged had completed about 270-degrees. Then with the pressure relaxed my eyesight returned and I peered rearwards to seek my aggressor. He was nowhere in sight, but then nor was the rest of my flight. The bombers had moved on and were hardly visible. Some combats were still raging high above me and I tried to gain height to join them, but they faded away before I could. Flitting inconclusively around for a while, I tried to identify from the radio calls where the rest of the squadron had got to but without success. Realising, as I was to find out with much emphasis later, that a single aircraft on its own is a liability, I returned to Kenley.

The next few scrambles did not produce much tangible success for the squadron. Our interceptions were being made at ever increasing altitudes which involved constant mix-ups with the Messerschmitt fighter cover. The actions developed into slueing dogfights where the opposing fighters found it difficult to get to lethal firing positions owing to the high speeds involved. Even when we engaged the lower covering formations, the fact that we were always heavily outnumbered meant that we constantly had to beware of more enemy fighters above us. As a mêlée developed and we tried to sort out a suitable target at our level or below, we would often be forced to turn into the fast attacks streaming down from the high cover. Ammunition was expended in numerous snap shots at fleeting targets with little result. Dog-fighting in the thin atmosphere above 20,000-feet was a tactic we had sadly never practised in our training because such measures had never been envisaged. But we learnt fast and the knowledge was shortly to stand us in very good stead.

Saturday, 7th September dawned on the most bizarre day in the squadron's history. Early in the morning, we were scrambled on a nervous controller's intuition. Whatever the reason for our despatch, there proved to be nothing to intercept. We were vectored back and forth over Kent chasing a mythical enemy, and after boring holes in the sky for an hour, pancaked back at Kenley. There followed a few hours' lull and alert states were relaxed. 66 was actually released from operations for the rest of the day which gave our hard-pressed ground crews a chance to catch up on servicing the aircraft. Pilots were not slow to react to this rare opportunity for a few hours off duty and our erstwhile leader, Rupert Leigh, filled his large Humber staff car with half a dozen of us whereupon we set off towards London for an evening on the town. Motivated by his sporting inclinations, Rupert headed first for Catford stadium where mid afternoon saw us resplendent in best uniforms busy backing the fortunes of reluctant greyhounds.

In the middle of the proceedings, the *Luftwaffe* launched its most massive air raid of the war. 350 bombers escorted by over 600 fighters advanced up the Thames estuary and blitzed the East End dock area just down the road from our Catford habitat.

The bombing was accurate. All along the docks from Rotherhithe to Tilbury, combustible materials in the warehouses erupted in raging fires, live ammunition and containers of nitroglycerine exploded at Woolwich Arsenal, and from the storage at Thameshaven the oil ignited into spectacular flames. A gigantic pall of brown-black smoke enshrouded the entire East End.

Twenty squadrons of Hurries and Spits tore into the invaders including a section of 66 whose pilots were still at Kenley when the raid started. These three, led by Bogle Bodie, got tangled up with a large number of Messerschmitt escorts resulting in Bodie getting shot up and being forced to crash-land in a field.

The noise was appaling as the tumult raged overhead. The crash of cascading bombs mingled with the incessant roar of artillery as our gunners blasted back. But nothing deterred the gambling instinct of the rugged London citizens. The dog races continued on schedule and the spirit of Drake reigned again.

From nought feet at the dog track, we gazed aghast at the holocaust. Rupert squinted up at the great phalanx of over a thousand milling aircraft and, as it wheeled away, collected his bunch of helpless fighter pilots. Quoth he: 'Chaps, I can't help feeling this is a case of Nero fiddling while Rome burns!' Unobtrusively we got the hell out of it.

The evening was well advanced and there was no time to get back to Kenley before dusk. Endowed with the press on spirit we decided to continue our sojourn and dodged through the chaos wrought in the aftermath of the raid to wind up in central London. An hour or so later, so did the *Luftwaffe*. Guided by the fierce glow of the burning fires from the afternoon's onslaught, the night bombers got to work on the Metropolis. The blitz had started; this was war with the lid off. We curtailed our foray and after a hair-raising journey through the turmoil south of the Thames, arrived back at the comparative bliss of Kenley.

CHAPTER FIVE

'GET IT RIGHT, OLD BOY'

'Get it right, old boy, otherwise don't bother'

Group Captain Sir Douglas Bader, CBE, DSO, DFC

The daylight offensive continued with increasing intensity. After the clobbering we had suffered in the few days since moving south, we had absorbed the hard lessons meted out. The squadron was now flying with mounting confidence, but the brunt of the fighting fell on the more experienced surviving pilots. In the two months since the battle started Fighter Command had sustained such heavy losses that the supply of trained fighter pilots was exhausted. Our replacements began to arrive from the Operational Training Units before they had finished their courses. They could only muster little more than 10-hours flying on a Spitfire which, though unavoidable, was grossly insufficient. With such a background they could scarcely fly the aircraft let alone fight with it. None had even fired their guns and tragically they became lambs for the slaughter. Within the next ten days seven of these chaps arrived to fill the gaps and none lasted more than three weeks.

After a hectic week at Kenley which seemed like a lifetime, the squadron moved to Gravesend and joined the Biggin Hill wing. 74 commanded by 'Sailor' Malan and 92 were the other two squadrons based on Biggin itself.

When we were not being scrambled on specific sorties to intercept identified raids, the long days were filled with defensive patrols over the vital approach routes to London. There was plenty of action and in the next few days the kills claimed by the squadron began to mount. Rupert Leigh, Dizzy Allen and Duggie Hunt all shot down a Heinkel each. I managed to single out a Dornier 17 over Seaford in Sussex and belted its engines, both of which were smoking as it disappeared diving steeply into cloud. I claimed this as damaged, but the next day the Royal Observer Corps confirmed it as crashing into the Channel off Beachy Head. After a scrap with 109's George Corbett was injured and baled out near Tunbridge Wells. Robbie Robbins and Sergeant Willcocks both got bounced and crash-landed, Robbie being seriously wounded.

The hectic actions filled the long days and we slipped into a routine. An hour before dawn we crawled out of bed, forced down some breakfast and got shaken into wakefulness as we were transported to dispersal in a hard-arsed lorry. We arrived to the cacophony of Merlin engines being warmed up and tested all round the airfield by the reliable fitters. Having chalked up the allocations of pilots to aircraft and formation compositions we donned our Mae West life jackets, collected our parachutes and helmets and trudged out to our aircraft. Detailed walk round inspections such as are the mode today would have been an insult to our conscientious ground crews, many of whom had been up all night rectifying faults and repairing battle damage. A quick kick on the tyres followed by a nervous pee on the rudder was quite sufficient.

The next move was to carefully arrange the safely harness and parachute straps, plug in the helmet leads to radio and oxygen so that on a scramble the least possible time would be lost in getting strapped in and away. Quick checks to see that the oxygen was flowing through the mask, that the gunsight was working with spare bulb in place and we were ready to go. As we fidgeted about with these essential tasks we exchanged facetious banter with our faithful ground crews. Very often in those autumn days there was a murky pre-dawn mist soaking the aircraft in heavy condensation which ran off the windscreen and cockpit canopy. We'd grab a rag from the rigger and

Lieutenant Robert Oxspring, King's Own Yorkshire Light Infantry. France 1915. Later Captain 54 & 66 Squadrons Royal Flying Corps 1916/17. He retired Major, Royal Air Force 1918; MC and Bar.

RWO in the cockpit of Spitfire Mark I K9986, Taken at RAF Wattisham, 2 July 1939.

66 Squadron, Duxford 1939. (Standing L to R) Rimmer, Smith, RWO, Paton, Campbell-Colquhoun, Grafstra, Brown, Kennard (Seated L to R) Power, Browne, Jago, Fuller-Good, Heath, Thomas, Gillies.

RWO and Tim Craxton. 66 Squadron, Duxford 1939.

RWO at RAF Duxford, winter 1939/40, wearing full Irvin suit.

RWO at Duxford, winter 1939/40.

Some of 66 Squadron, Gravesend 1940. (L to R) Reilley, Bodie, Christie, Leigh, Watkinson, RWO, Alien.

66 Squadron, Duxford 1940. Frankie Rimmer and RWO.

Ken Gillies, 66 Squadron, Gravesend 1940

Johnnie Johnson, 616 Squadron, Tangmere 1940.

Some of 66 Squadron, Gravesend 1940. {L to R} RWO, Leigh, Gillies, Watkinson, Allen, Hewitt (adjutant), Hutton (IO), Reilley.

Leutnant *Erich Bodendiek*

66 Squadron, Gravesend 1940. George Corbett, F/0 Davis (M0) and Ken Gillies.

Frankie Rimmer.

Bogle Bodie and Durex Kendal, Gravesend 1940.

RWO at Biggin Hill, November 1940.

RWO, 66 Squadron, Biggin Hill, November 1940.

91 Squadron at Hawkinge 1942 (L to R) 'Diamond Jim' Brady RWO and F/0 Ely.

HRH The Duke of Kent and Dicky Barwell, Biggin Hill 1942.

Joy Oxspring, RWO and General Adolf Galland at Biggin Hill 1964.

help him polish the transparent areas as clear as we could get them. We had learned the hard way that unrestricted visibility was vital to fighter pilots whose aggression and indeed survival depended so much on clarity of vision.

Pre-flight checks completed, we sloped off back to the crew room and settled down to a fighter pilot's day which somebody aptly described as long periods of intense boredom punctuated by moments of sheer terror.

We lounged around the dispersal talking, playing cards or just sitting. Periodically the telephone rang jerking us all into boggle-eyed alertness. More often than not the telephone orderly would call one of us to answer some innocuous administrative call and the tension of another anticipated order to combat receded. That telephone played hell with our nerves. I don't think any of us pilots ever again appreciated the virtues of Mr Bell's invention. Sooner or later though, the action charged instruction came through. The orderly would pause, listen and then bawl:

'Squadron scramble, Maidstone. Angels two zero.'

Before he'd relayed the message we were away sprinting to our Spitfires. As we ran the fitters fired the starter cartridges and the propellers turned with engines roaring into life. From strapping in to chocks away was a matter of seconds. Taxiing to the take-off point on the broad grass airfield took even less time. Pausing to let the last aircraft get roughly in position, the squadron commander's upraised hand signal then came down and twelve pilots gunned their throttles speeding away on the take-off in a wide vie formation of flights.

As the squadron got airborne canopies snapped shut and wheels sucked into the wells. The leader's voice crackled in the earphones: 'Rastus, Fibus airborne.'

The controller's response immediate: 'Roger, Fibus Leader, one hundred plus bandits south of Ashford heading north west angels one five. Vector 130, Buster.'

Buster meant the fastest speed attainable. The squadron commander held the maximum power setting he could afford to ensure that the rest of the squadron had a slight margin of speed to keep up with him. Cutting the corners on every variation of the leader's heading the flights gradually slid into the climb formation of sections line astern.

Struggling to gain every inch of height in the shortest possible time we gradually emerged out of the filthy brown haze which perpetually hung like a blanket over London. Suddenly, around 12,000-feet we broke through the smog layer and a different world emerged, startling in its sun-drenched clarity.

Long, streaming contrails snaked way above us from the Channel coast as the Messerschmitt high-flying fighters weaved protectively over their menacing bomber formations. Our radios became almost unintelligible as pilots in our numerous intercepting squadrons called out sightings, attack orders, warnings and frustrated oaths. Green 2 and 3, our two weavers who criss-crossed above the squadron formation, took up their stations to guard against attacks from the vulnerable blind area behind. Somehow a familiar voice of any one of our pilots would break through the radio chatter with an urgent, 'Fibus Leader, bandits eleven o'clock level.'

The CO's aircraft instantly started to take up an initial attack position as his voice responded, 'Fibus Leader, Tally Ho; Fibus aircraft echelon starboard. Go.'

Interception of the enemy almost always developed this way, but the ensuing action depended on variable circumstances of the time: the position of the bombers, the proximity of enemy fighters, the manoeuvrings of our fellow squadrons, our height advantage or otherwise over our targets and a host of factors which dictated our immediate tactics.

The Group Commander's basic strategy was to direct his more numerous Hurricane squadrons on to the enemy bomber formations at the same time hopefully providing protective cover for them from his faster Spitfire squadrons. Often this plan fell down because for various reasons our interceptors engaged at slightly different times and which, if only a minute apart, could spoil any intended co-ordination. At the same time the primary objective of the RAF defenses was the destruction of enemy bombers. The Messerschmitts were unable to inflict any primary damage except to our defending fighters. Frequently our squadron would plummet into an attack on the bomber formations, but the fast reacting German fighter cover headed in to cut us off. This usually resulted in our leading flight getting in amongst the bombers whilst we in B flight had to turn into the attacking 109's coming at us from the rear. From that moment our squadron cohesion broke up. Flights split into sections, battle with the enemy was joined, and in the following violent manoeuvres the sections broke down into pairs and often single aircraft. Multiple and single combats rippled out across the sky as opposing fighters locked into deadly conflict. Squadrons which had managed to get among the bombers closed in their attacks to point blank range. Breaking away they used their superior speed to climb out on the flanks and seek opportunities to set up renewed passes. Again our formations whittled down to sections and these in turn became vulnerable to the greatly superior numbers of the German fighter staffels who peeled down from their advantageous altitudes above.

Flak shells from our anti-aircraft batteries below winked in and around the enemy armadas. The lingering smoke from the bursts tracked the invaders' course and made it easy for those pilots breaking off dog fights to pick up the centre of action again. At all heights the combats milled, the sun glinting on wings over which staccato bursts of grey gunsmoke streamed back into the slipstream as opposing fighter pilots strove to nail each other.

Stricken aircraft littered the sky and depleted bomber formations heralded the carnage inflicted by our fighters. Spiralling plumes of dirty smoke marked the death dives of savagely hit Heinkels and Dorniers. Battle-damaged bombers strove to keep up with their formations or straggled to the flanks to be set upon by vengeful Hurries and Spits. Here and there the horizon was dissected by black trails of flaming fighters as victims on both sides fell out of the sky. British and German parachutes floated down in all directions as the battle reached its climax.

The incessant harrying of the bomber fleets by our fighters had varying effects. If we were lucky enough to knock out some of the leading aircraft, the formations would begin to break up. Bombs were jettisoned and the survivors would wheel around and head back towards France. But most times the resolute German commanders pressed on with their battered formations to their targets. Then they too turned for home, speeding up their bomb-lightened aircraft to beat a hasty retreat. With their covering fighters at maximum range and low on fuel, the enemy air fleets were now at their most vulnerable stage. Conjointly, it provided opportunity for reinforcing fighters from 10 and 12 Groups to intercept from their distant airfields. Soon a running battle flowed across southern England the intensity of which depended on the amount of ammunition the opposing fighters had left.

Ammunition dominated every fighter pilot's life. With it he was lethal; without it he was useless. Sooner or later he would expend his ten seconds of fire power and then was the time to retire from the battle.

Back at base the aircraft returned in one's and two's – most of them, that is. Sometimes one or more Spits were missing. Our loyal ground crews kept tally of the planes as they swept into the circuit, ready as always with oxygen, fuel and ammunition to 'turn the kites round quick'. Rarely did they exceed twelve minutes for a whole squadron. Watching 'their' pilots touch down, grins spread across faces as they heard the whine of exposed gun ports singing the message that bullets had fired in anger. Those whose pilots did not return hung around their vacant dispersals and gazed dejectedly at an empty sky.

The mission completed, pilots ambled back to the crew room, completed the debrief, in some cases stopped a rocket from the CO or flight commanders for some piece of poor airmanship, and then grabbed something to eat. One by one the aircraft were reported back as turned round. Spare Spitfires and pilots, if any, were chalked up on the operations board and the squadron reported back to readiness.

The high tension and excitement generated throughout the squadron gradually receded. Pilots' sweat-ridden shirts dried out, and stomachs returned to normal. If this had been a morning show, we all knew that there could be at least two more formidable raids to contest before the day was through. Occasionally the activity called for five scrambles in the hours of daylight, but some were false alarms and not all resulted in combat. A quick visit to our aircraft for the usual cockpit check and we'd settle down with some apprehension to await the next call to action.

Sunday, 15th September closely followed this pattern of events and that particular day is now generally accepted as the climax of the Battle of Britain. Erroneously believing that the air war of attrition over the previous nine weeks had reduced the RAF's fighter force to 'the last fifty Spitfires', the *Luftwaffe* commanders threw everything they had into two massive raids on London.

In mid-morning the first assault crossed the coast at Dungeness. 66 scrambled with other 11 Group squadrons to intercept near Maidstone, and despite the heavy Messerschmitt cover, we managed to get in among a formation of Heinkel 111 's. B flight was the last to attack and we selected the nearest vic of bombers. Firing a long deflection burst on my target without any apparent result, I broke down underneath and then up and away to the side. George Corbett stuck with me and whilst deciding the next move we saw a solitary Spitfire ahead of us. It was Ken Gillies, and as we joined up with him he recognised my markings and called, 'Hang on, Bobby, we'll shake this lot up.' He led us forward and then turned round into a head on attack. Flying line abreast we fired all the way in to point blank range on the leading vic of Heinkels.

As we broke down and away beneath our targets we saw the formation had separated. But the main stream still advanced on London and at that moment we witnessed the glorious sight of five squadrons from the Duxford wing, led by Douglas Bader, come sailing into the raid. The impact of a further sixty Hurricanes and Spitfires charging in on the already sorely harassed bomber fleet was too much. Bombs were jettisoned indiscriminately on south-east London, and the raiders fled for home.

The afternoon's party was even more impressive. A large gaggle of Dorniers and Heinkels with the usual formidable fighter escort moved in towards London and 66 was vectored on to them. The hostile fleet was stacked up to about 17,000-feet where A flight dropped on a high-flying formation of Heinkels. As we in B flight started to follow, a flight of 109's appeared about 1,000-feet above and behind us. Fearing they might jump us we turned towards them, but an attack did not develop. We continued our turn and closed in on the bombers which we pressed hard enough to persuade one of them to part company with his mates. Harried by the flight the Heinkel dived for sanctuary in the cloud layer below, but just before he reached it he gave up the struggle and lowered his wheels. Escorted by a covey of buzzing Spits he landed at West Malling.

Starting to climb to regain height, I noticed some flak bursts behind me surrounding a Dornier 17 which for some odd reason was flying north. It was climbing for the cloud layer, but I caught it before it got there and belted the fuselage in a rake of fire down to very close range. Two crew members parachuted out, followed shortly afterwards by two more. The Dornier spiralled into a dive and crashed on a house in Rochester. Rupert

Leigh saw all this happen and after we landed expressed his vexation at not being close enough to have a go himself.

Being most concerned as to the fate of any of the house occupants when my Dornier arrived through their roof, I checked with the police. I was relieved to be told that nobody had been hurt since the place was unoccupied at the time. Mercifully the lady owner and her small son were down the road sharing a neighbour's shelter. As a sequel to this, some twenty-eight years after, I attended an official Battle of Britain function at the Birmingham City Hall which called for number one uniform. This included a sword which I did not possess. Accordingly the RAF arranged to supply one and this was brought to me by an officer from Cosford. He turned out to be Flight Lieutenant Don Christmas, the former small boy occupant of the ill-fated house in Rochester. He said he could not pass up the opportunity to meet me, and that he and his mother held no recriminations for my rendering them homeless all those years before.

As the evening of 15th September lengthened the English skies cleared of aircraft. Reports were coming in thai Fighter Command had achieved a major victory. On 66 Dizzy Allen, Duggie Hunt and Sergeant Parsons each claimed a Heinkel 111; Ken Gillies, Bogie Bodie and I all registered with Dornier 17's. It was all on the plus side since we had no casualties.

The events of the afternoon raid were witnessed by Prime Minister Winston Churchill in the Operations Room at 11 Group. As our squadrons rose to meet the assault he made his famous query: 'What reserves have we got?' and was told there were none. Indeed, at least twenty-five squadrons got to grips with the enemy.

The *Luftwaffe* returned to the continent to lick its wounds. Morale must have been deeply shattered that 'the last fifty Spitfires' had turned out to be a confrontation of over 300 aggressive Hurries and Spits barring the path of their maximum effort assaults.

Buoyed up with our success, we waited a repeat performance the following day. It didn't come. The German struggle for air supremacy had failed. In the meantime, night after night throughout the previous month, Bomber and Coastal Commands had hammered away with great success on the invasion barges assembled in the French and Belgian ports. Hitler postponed operation 'Sealion'. It was destined never to be launched.

CHAPTER SIX

'Don't panic, I've got 'em surrounded!'

Pilot Officer C A W 'Bogle' Bodie, DFC

They say variety is the spice of life but sometimes that's hard to believe. Early one morning a section of B flight was ordered to Hawkinge for an unspecified mission. Dizzy and Pickles joined me and we were met for briefing by the station commander on an ops order from HQ 11 Group. Our task was to escort an obsolete Avro Anson to Calais which was to spot the fall of Royal Artillery shells from the long range guns at Dover; one shell to be fired every fifteen minutes over the period of an hour.

We couldn't believe our ears. This was the most asinine and utterly futile operational order I ever received in the entire war. But orders are orders and we pressed on across the Channel into hostile airspace. Our charge and its apprehensive but courageous crew extracted every ounce of power from the ancient Cheetah engines. If they hit 120-mph it was pushing it, and the assigned altitude of 10,000-feet was nudging the operational ceiling.

We tottered over Calais at zero hour when presumably the first shell arrived from Dover. It was not recorded whether the crew pinpointed the fall, but we retreated out to sea and then returned fifteen minutes later for the second shot. This time we sighted six or more German fighters climbing up sun some miles to the south. Not being in radio contact with the Anson we used the prearranged warning signal by rocking our wings. The Anson pilot needed no further urging and headed back for Hawkinge as fast as the old beast would fly. In retrospect it is unbelievable that Fighter Command with an acute shortage of Spitfires and pilots could hazard its resources on such a pointless mission. Had the German fighters intercepted us, we would all have been sitting ducks.

After shepherding our Anson safety to Hawkinge we said farewell and hurried back to Gravesend. A further four operations were to be flown that day on the last of which my section forced a Heinkel 111 to crash land on Walland Marsh where it took fire on impact.

The next few days disclosed a noticeable change in German strategy. The very large bomber fleets no longer threatened in daylight. Except for scattered tilts the *Luftwaffe* had largely withdrawn its fleet of Heinkel Ill's and Dornier 17's from daylight raids. This force concentrated its efforts in maintaining the night blitz on the capital and other cities. Despite its failure to attain air superiority over southern England, the Luftwaffe nevertheless stepped up its activity against Fighter Command. Fewer but much faster Junkers 88 bombers, together with the two seat Messerschmitt 110's which were now fitted with two 500-kg bombs were thrown into the fray. This latter twin-engined fighter had met with disastrous casualties when contemptuously out-manoeuvred by our single seat fighters in previous weeks but, with adequate escort, it was apparently considered to have the speed to perform hit and run raids. In fact the German fighter squadrons were increasingly to be found without any bomber bait at all. They freelanced over southern England enticing Fighter Command into action.

Such a radical change in strategy called for an equal rethink of tactics on our part. The previous urgent requirement for us to intercept the incoming raids at the earliest opportunity was no longer so paramount. We could now afford to take the time to get to high altitude and build up our speed before engaging the enemy. Paradoxically the delay could cause us to miss the intercept, but it was better to be too late than to get bounced on the climb. But to eliminate the time lost in the climb from a scramble, we were now increasingly flying patrols just inland of the coast. Often we were in squadron strength but occasionally this was beefed up to a wing of two squadrons.

In effect, the marauding fighter staffels were operating as hunting packs, and their formation numbers varied from half a dozen or so to *Geschwaders* of 200 plus. But we had news for them; freed from our 'backs to the wall' role against the bomber menace, we were hunting too.

Only three days before the epic Sunday we were on patrol with 92 Squadron from Biggin Hill. This outfit had enjoyed considerable success in the previous few weeks and was composed of a varied bunch of characters, some of whom seemed to regard the war as an extended furlough from the flesh-pots of Mayfair. Brian Kingcome, Pancho Villa, Wimpy Wade, Allan Wright, Tony Bartley, Don Kingaby, Tich Havercroft and Bob Holland are to mention but a few who had already made their mark in the air, and were to go on to greater things later in the war.

Our two squadrons, having staggered up to 30,000 feel were riding a line north of Dover when we sighted a flight of 109's converging on 92 Squadron and our CO called a warning. 92's Spitfires turned under the attack which continued over them towards us. 66's leading section climbed after one of the enemy, and I led my section after another. Dizzy Allen, my number two, covered my tail as I attacked from the starboard side and below. After two short bursts my victim burst into flames and as it dived away the pilot baled out. The aircraft reeled on down to smack into east Kent somewhere north of Folkestone.

Over forty years afterwards, air historian Flying Officer Chris Goss RAF introduced me to my victim on this sortie, Leutnant Erich Bodendiek, then a fighter pilot with *Jagdgeschwader* 53 - the famous 'Pik As' (Ace of Spades) Group. Bodendiek tells me ruefully that this was a particularly unfortunate day for him. In his capacity as technical officer on the 4th *Staffel* he was flying one of the newly modified Me 109's with a variable pitch propeller. When his formation crossed the English coast the pitch mechanism failed and he was stuck with a prop at a fixed angle. This restricted his speed particularly in the climb, and he was unable to reach the cover of the high cirrus as the others of his flight had done when we attacked.

Interestingly, his account of the action tallies almost exactly with my combat report in height, place and the resultant activities. When he baled out he was slightly burnt but not seriously, and he parachuted down to land in the sea a couple of miles off Folkestone. An air sea rescue launch picked him up to take him prisoner of war. After sojourns in England and Canada it was seven years before he returned to Germany.

At the end of my attack on Bodendiek I was hanging on my prop and my speed was so slow that my Spit was verging on a spin. A short dive regained the speed and we climbed up again. The other 109's had momentarily disappeared in a thick layer of cirrus cloud, but shortly afterwards four of them reappeared slightly above us. Two came after me and two after Dizzy who managed to get out of the way. I faced my first attacker and got in two bursts as he turned past. Some bits flew off him, one of which Dizzy afterwards said was his canopy. Seeing some tracer flicking past on my right I saw another 109 behind me and had to break into a smart turn away. Suddenly there was nothing left in sight and we high tailed it home. Bodendiek says there were eighteen Me 109's on this mission, yet we only saw a flight.

Although most of the enemy activity was generated by the fast-flying Messerschmitts and Junkers 88's, the Heinkels and Dorniers were still being used on singleton reconnaissance sorties when the weather favoured them. One such day was heavy with thick haze and mist but Biggin Hill ops managed to vector my section on to a Heinkel 111 some miles north of Hastings at 19,000-feet. As I closed in to range with my No 2, Pilot Officer Hugh Reilley, the Heinkel made off in a shallow dive. We fired in turn at the engines which both emitted smoke. Shortly afterwards it disappeared into the haze and we claimed it as a probable. Something disastrous must have occurred aboard because some days later we heard it had been confirmed as having crashed between Maidstone and Gravesend. All the crew were killed.

Friday, 27th September, erupted into a vicious series of fast running raids by Ju 88's and bomb-carrying Me 110's; these attacks penetrated the coast from Dover to Portland, their targets being a number of our aircraft factories in the south. 66 Squadron was vectored off patrol to intercept a raid returning from the Croydon area. We sighted ten Me 110's heading south at 16,000-feet being harassed by some Hurricanes. Splitting into sections we went straight in to attack. The 110's started a defensive mill but it was not well coordinated and the action broke up into a series of scraps. I sighted one 110 coming up in a violent climb followed by a Hurricane about 300-yards behind. Reaching the top of his climb and practically on the stall, the 110 was almost a stationary target. I let fly with a longish burst and his port engine spurted out flames as he fell into a spin. Nobody baled out and it thumped into the ground a few miles south of Biggin Hill. Somewhere these 110's had lost their 109 escort and took a severe thrashing with 66 and the Hurricanes of 46 Squadron having the lion's share.

Furious actions followed one after the other throughout the day and we were scrambled twice more. Having missed our interception on the first, the second brought some hectic fighting as we ran into a formation of 88's escorted by a cloud of 109's near Ashford. As A flight fell on the 88's, a number of 109's streamed down to intercept. We in B flight turned into them and a desperate dogfight followed. We milled around snap shooting at fleeting targets interposed with savage breaks into dangerous attacks from behind. As the conflict spread and faded we hurried home to assess the damage. It was quite a day. Dizzy Allen got a 109, Sergeants Parsons and Cameron each claimed a Ju 88 and Ken Gillies with his flight accounted for three more. George Corbett knocked down another Ju 88 but was then hit by a burst of our own flak and had to crash-land near Orpington.

Casualties on both sides had been heavy. Apart from George's prang, we were unscathed, but we learnt on the grapevine that our two ex-stalwarts Bill Smith and Frankie Rimmer, both flight commanders on 229 Squadron, had been clobbered by 109's. Bill succeeded in crash-landing, but Frankie went in with his Hurricane.

The *Luftwaffe* persisted in its freelancing raids over southern England and a few days later in company with 92 Squadron we caught one running in near Sevenoaks. As 92 went after the 88's, we charged into a flight of 109's which were moving in to intercept. They streamed across our front and we picked our targets. Mine obligingly moved into my gunsight and got what he deserved. He staggered up into a steep climb and then rolled on to his back and dived away emitting spurts of flame and smoke from the underside of his engine. He disappeared leaving a smoky trail behind him a little way south of Biggin Hill. It was impossible to follow him as there were still thirty or more 109's to keep us occupied as the raid withdrew.

Since Frankie Rimmer had been a particular friend of mine and I knew his family, I asked Rupert Leigh if I could attend the funeral. Rupert not only agreed but asked me to take a wreath from the squadron. Accordingly I took my Spit with the wreath strapped behind the seat and headed off for Liverpool. Frankie's father, Lance, was ex-Royal Flying Corps and had continued flying since World War I. In the thirties he had barnstormed with Alan Cobham's Circus, but was now chief production test pilot on Bristol Blenheims which were being produced at Speke. When I got there Lance hangared my Spitfire in his factory shed and after the funeral I stayed the night at his house. The next morning when the Spit was wheeled out I found it to be smothered with 'good luck' signatures in pencil, ink and chalk. Wings and fuselage were covered and surely every employee at the factory had scribed his moniker. It was a memorable gesture but my conscientious rigger wasn't over-enamoured when he next saw old X4170. I told him he mustn't tempt fate and clean off all those good wishes.

On return to Gravesend it was distressing to be told that Ken Gillies was missing. Only that morning the squadron had been in action and as the scattered pilots were returning to base Ken was heard to call that he had been hit but that he thought he could get back to the airfield. He didn't make it and two weeks later his body was washed up at Covehithe. We could only conclude that the problems with his aircraft were serious enough to force him to bale out over the sea, but not knowing where he was, we couldn't mount a search. His loss was a grievous blow to our morale; the feeling was, 'If Ken bought it, what chance have we peons got?'

It did not take long to gain some revenge for Ken. Next morning the squadron was vectored on to a hostile raid near Maidstone around 20,000-feet. Half a dozen spasmodic anti-aircraft shell bursts drew our attention to a *staffel* of Me 109's flying south-eastwards from London. They were about our height as we initiated a streaming attack on them. The enemy were flying in loose pairs which broke formation as we closed into firing range. One yellow-nosed 109 broke left to right across my front and I got a nice three-seconds burst on it from behind and beneath. He turned through the hazy sun as I repeated the dose which resulted in a stream of grey smoke.

The aircraft dived down and I followed firing from close range. The rudder flew off and almost instantaneously the aircraft burst into flames. Our hurtling descent carried us uncomfortably close to a squadron of Hurricanes concentrating on a climb out. I had to giggle when our sudden spectacular arrival from aloft split the Hurries' formation which cascaded in all directions. In striving to avoid ramming one of my startled friends I managed to glimpse the 109 spinning on down near Lympne. There was no sign of a parachute, but later records listed the pilot, *Feldwebel* Pankratz of *Lehrgeschwader* 2, as missing. In the running fight into which the action developed, the 109's damaged three of 66's Spitfires flown by Wright, Bodie and Kendal, the last of whom was slightly wounded.

As time passed it was evident that the enemy had largely dispensed with the bomber escort routine, and the opposition was mainly free-ranging Me 109 fighter sweeps over the southern counties. Trying to intercept one of these raids one day, we were caught on the climb at 20,000-feet over the Medway. Flying a fairly loose formation, I had my No 2 George Corbett on my right. Nobody saw the bounce, and I just happened to glance at George when to my horror I saw his aircraft explode in flames. Fractionally later, I saw a 109 close behind him still firing. I broke violently over the top of George expecting the same treatment, but if another 109 was there I didn't see it. George didn't stand a chance and a few days later this gallant Canadian was buried nearby where he fell at Upchurch, such a long way from his native Vancouver. Later in the day A flight was similarly jumped and the promising Sergeant Ward was killed.

The month of October wore on with hectic skirmishes occurring almost daily. Whenever possible we gained maximum height before getting committed. These contests in the rarefied air presented their own peculiar difficulties in manoeuvring to bring our sights to bear. Aircraft had to be flown much more gingerly because any excessive G force invited an incipient stall which could precede a spin leading to a loss of precious altitude.

One exhausting day involved us in prolonged scraps starting around 30,000-feet and inevitably the combats worked down to lower altitudes. Having lost height on one of these inconclusive mills I collected some of my flight together and prepared to climb back to the action.

Bodie elected to weave above the rest of us as look out and suddenly he called: 'Give me a hand, Bob, I've got a problem.' I'd lost sight of him for a moment and said: 'OK, where are you?

As he replied the gravity of his predicament was emphasised by the wheezing of heavy breathing in the backtone of his mike:

'Hurwheez, six o'clock high.'

Then I spotted him a couple of thousand feet up in the middle of half a dozen 109's desperately reefing around and fighting for his life. We poured on the coals as I called, 'Hang on, Bogle, we've got to get some height.' In fully fine pitch we practically stood on our tails and just to encourage him I transmitted: 'Be with you in a minute, Bogle.'

Back came his comment: 'Hurwheez, don't panic, I've got 'em surrounded!'

We staggered into the mêlée with practically no forward speed, but our sudden appearance diverted the 109s' attention from Bodie because they broke the engagement. Our speed was too slow for us to give effective chase except for Bodie, who fastened on to one. He gave it the hammer and despatched his tormentor into a Kentish field. Bodie was a natural fighter pilot; aggressive, tenacious and tough, he would take on any odds and usually did. Son of an Essex dentist, it was sad that his life was wasted when he died in an accident to his Spitfire the following year.

October kept us so busy that time flashed by. When the squadron was released at dusk there was little opportunity to relax except to have a few beers at the local pubs. Favourites among these were the Leather Bottle at Cobham which somehow produced the most marvellous meals despite the food rationing, and the Ship near the docks in Gravesend. The latter's regular clients were the dockers and stevedores from the port who treated us so generously that it became embarrassing; we could never return a drink except by devious and surreptitious means. 66 was regarded as 'their' fighter squadron and 'their' exclusive defenders. When Hugh Reilley was buried they and their families turned out in large numbers to pay their respects as the cortege went by.

In the middle of the month we were very sorry to lose on posting our incomparable CO Rupert Leigh, whose humour and leadership had kept our morale sky high. His place was taken by Athol Forbes who came to us from the bloodthirsty 303 Polish Squadron at Northolt.

The vengeful 109's continued their daily sweeps across the south coast, and one afternoon ops pulled us off a patrol line at Maidstone to intercept a *Staffel* of three flights streaming in out of the sun. We were staggering along at 31,000-feet and had a couple of thousand feet height advantage which set up a nice bounce for us. Being of roughly equal numbers, we selected our targets and dropped off the perch. Our speed advantage was so great I had to throttle back to keep behind mine. After my first burst he dived and we belted on downhill. His heading directly followed the dead straight Tonbridge to Ashford railway line which I suppose pointed his way home.

Around 12,000-feet he pulled out and started a climb which enabled me to shorten the range and let him have another dose. Unfortunately only my starboard guns were working so he didn't get the full treatment, but it was enough to encourage him to continue down. I fired a couple of more bursts before my windscreen iced up and I lost sight of him down at tree level. After searching around in the ground haze for a bit I called it off and went home. Later that evening, it was satisfying to be told that he had crash-landed in a field six miles east of Ashford.

We pilots were living under considerable tension. Each of us wondered when it would be our turn to stop a pack of lead. The 25th October duly obliged as my red letter day.

I was leading B flight on a standing patrol in the Maidstone area. The six of us had been airborne for nearly an hour when Biggin Hill control alerted us to a six plus hostile raid approaching North Foreland and vectored us eastward to intercept it. We were flying at 30,000-feet, which was just about maximum altitude for station keeping in battle formation, and as we approached the coast we sighted an enemy gaggle coming inland towards Canterbury.

I counted six Messerschmitt 109 E's in loose line abreast and their heading was taking them beneath us in the opposite direction. For the first line in the conflict we had all the advantage. We were up sun, we had superior height, we were equal in number and it appeared that they hadn't yet seen us. I put the flight into line astern and ordered the attack advising that there was one for each of us. We peeled down in the bounce and I homed in on the leader. I was just getting in to maximum range of about 500-yards when they saw us and my target bunted down into a steep dive. Since hopefully the rest of B flight following me down had selected their victims, I stuck with my 109 and slowly got more into shooting range. We were creaming downhill and I could feel the high speed buffeting on the elevators and the ailerons stiffening up. I was considering whether to open fire or get closer in when all hell broke loose.

Something smashed into the fuselage behind me with an arse-twitching crash and I ducked my head, a somewhat futile reaction when it's too late anyway. It was something I'd been half expecting for the past two months but when it arrived it surpassed all expectations. The stick felt loose in my hand and there was no elevator control. Whatever trim forces were left were certainly of the nose-up variety because despite my pushing the useless pole, the Spit violently rounded out of the dive and soared viciously into an upward zoom.

The resulting G forces blacked me out and I was helplessly pinned down in the seat. Evidently the uncontrolled gyrations followed that of the looping plane because the G's eased off and as my eyeballs refocussed I saw I was inverted with the aircraft pitching down again into another dive. I confess that near panic took over and I started actions for baling out. I flipped out the Sutton harness locking pin and reached for the canopy opening bar, but once again the aircraft hit the base of the dive and hurtled into another climb as I blacked out once more. Again I come to in a near inverted attitude as I strove frantically to open the canopy but without success.[2]

The next time the pressure eased off, I was in a stalled position with the nose pointing at the sky and I realised that in the flap I had not throttled back the engine. Quickly I yanked back the power and as the speed of the next dive decreased I was again able to struggle with the canopy. Finally with one big heave it shot back and I tried to stand up. I stuck my head out into the slipstream, but found myself still tied to the aircraft by my RT lead and oxygen tube so I leant back down and ripped my helmet off.

As I did so my desire to part company with dear old X4170 was

---

[2] In 1940 Spitfires had not yet been fitted with the emergency canopy ejectio release, and opening the standard canopy became progressively more difficull as the airspeed increased.

enhanced as I saw flames spreading along the cockpit floor between the rudder bars. Whatever the reason for the fire, either a fizzing incendiary shell, or more likely an ignition in the oil tank, it was obviously time to depart. The Spit was starting to dive again as I strove to get upright and as my shoulders cleared the cockpit I was plucked out into space.

The initial sensation was one of profound relief. The feel of the cool air after the sweaty struggle in the hot cockpit was most refreshing. In my desperate efforts to get out I had no idea how near the ground I was because the whole action seemed to have taken an age in time so without delay I grabbed the D ring and pulled it.

But hasty action does not always bring the best results, and when the ripcord released the pilot chute, I was dropping head first backwards at an angle of about forty-five degrees. The canopy and shroud lines streamed out between my legs and as they did so one of the lines wrapped round my left ankle and strung me upside down. To regain contact with England on my head did not appeal so I wriggled around to try and free my foot. Somehow, after hauling myself up one of the shrouds, I succeeded. As I cartwheeled right way up I fell with all my weight on to my testicles which, due to my frantic contortions, had got themselves adjacent to one of the leg loops of the harness. This was instant agony, but even then my troubles weren't over because the shrouds and shoulder webbings had become well and truly knotted just above my head.

With the webbing rasping against my face, I managed to loosen the knots a little and shake out the shrouds. This eased matters a bit but the twisted rigging restricted the deployment of the canopy to about half its proper area and I dropped earthwards at a considerably higher rate of knots than the norm.

Passing some scattered cumulus cloud I peered down between my legs and saw Tunbridge Wells beneath. I'd never been to this illustrious resort before, but it seemed that this circumstance was about to be rectified from on high. After the tumult of the cockpit, the quietness of the atmosphere was most striking, punctuated as it was only by the faint howls of engines and the chatter of machine guns from the dog fight still raging above.

Over in the distance and somewhat below me, I could see a couple of parachutes whose occupants had suffered much the same fate as myself. I sincerely hoped they were German and that my boys in B flight had done their stuff. I took another look at my tangled parachute and realised that with the speed of my fall I was going to hit the deck pretty hard, and at the very least would probably break my legs. Scanning the sky to see what next might befall me, I noticed with some alarm that my two parachuting cohorts were now above me and that I'd passed them on the descent which confirmed my suspicion that my rate of fall was a good deal more rapid than it should have been. These quandaries inspired a sudden devout Christianity as I earnestly sought Divine Guidance to steer me toward a friendly tree or lake which might just cushion the impending impact.

Fortune smiled and provided me with a whole wood just north of Pembury, and after a dodgy float over some high tension cables I crashed down through the foliage of an enormous tree. I covered my face with my arms as I went through the branches, and the canopy caught on the top of the tree leaving me suspended like a yoyo some twenty feet up. I managed to swing to one side and clamber up on to a branch still tied up in my harness. I didn't have long to wait before a number of the splendid and alert Home Guard arrived to the rescue and whisked me away to the Kent and Sussex General Hospital for a check-up. There the super medical staff gave me a sympathetic going over, produced a most welcome four fingers of brandy and pronounced me fit for further adventures.

Before I left I was asked to go along to one of the wards to see a badly injured pilot who hadn't been as lucky as me. I greatly regret I do not remember his name, but the poor chap had baled out of a blazing Hurricane about a month before and had suffered terrible burns. His hands and whole face were covered with bandages and he was still hoping he had not gone blind. I tried to talk facetious shop to him and he responded with a humour which belied the dreadful agony he was enduring. As I left he wished me luck. I felt very humble.

My inelegant arrival back in Kent marked the end of my trusty Spitfire X4170 which had carried me through the previous eventful weeks without a hiccup. The solicitous greetings from the good factory workers at Speke had paid off. It was virtually at the closure of the Battle of Britain which faded out as the winter encroached and gave us a respite. November saw us move to Biggin Hill to join 74 and 92 Squadrons.

Just to remind us that all was not finished the *Luftwaffe* elected to stage a spectacular end of term party at Dover. On 14th November a large gaggle of Ju 87 Stukas were incomprehensibly resurrected to bomb the port facilities escorted by numerous 109's. In company with 74 Squadron, we caught them on the approach and a savage battle was joined resulting in severe carnage among the Stukas. As usual my flight got mixed up with the 109 escort without any definite claims, but this left the way clear for the rest to get stuck in. Dizzy Allen accounted for one Stuka, but the lion's share went to 74 Squadron among whom Colin Mungo-Park, Steve H M Stephen and Bill Skinner devastated no less than seven between them. It was a fitting finale to 1940.

CHAPTER SEVEN

'THERE THEY GO'

'There they go, and I must hasten to catch up with them,
for I am their leader!'

Air Force Parody

The winter of 1940/41 socked in – operational flying was restricted to occasional operational patrols and a few scrambles. The lack of activity gave us a chance to give the new pilots some concentrated training and at the same time pay some overdue attention to the weaknesses in our tactics which had become evident during the hectic clashes with the German fighters.

We were fortunate that 'Sailor' Malan was still at Biggin Hill with his 74 'Tiger' Squadron. Sailor had emerged as the most successful fighter pilot in the Battle of Britain. He had quickly realised that the standardized formations in which we had been trained since long before the war were utterly unsuitable for the most successful fighting tactics against the 109's. Our close formations of basics vics of three had been designed for use against unescorted bombers as, understandably, the operation planning staffs had never envisaged the situation brought about by the fall of France whereby the short range 109's would be in easy reach of Britain.

The German fighter leaders used tactics evolved from their experience in Spain and flew in loose, easily manoeuverable flights based on the *Schwarm* of four aircraft. Sailor adopted basically the same tactics with 74 using a squadron formation of three flights in wide vic each with their four aircraft in line astern. It provided much greater freedom of action and the vastly improved cross-cover considerably reduced the chances of getting bounced from behind. Knowing the Tigers' record of high scores and low casualties the other squadrons quickly adopted Sailor's tactics and in so doing were significantly to improve the RAF's fighter aggressiveness and effectiveness throughout the forthcoming theatres of war. Over at Duxford, Douglas Bader was working on similar lines based on the 'finger four' formations which were almost identical to those employed by the *Luftwaffe*.

Apart from his battle formation theories Sailor enlightened us on his other principles of fighter combat which in the following year were produced in an Air Ministry pamphlet called *Malan's Ten Rules of Air Fighting*. It became a basic criterion for all fighter pilots.

At the turn of the year the new Commander-in-Chief, Air Marshal Sholto Douglas, altered Fighter Command's strategy. His aim was to take the offensive to the Germans and try to keep the *Luftwaffe* busy away from English shores on the other side of the Channel, The severe winter weather kept action to a minimum, but several operations in wing strength were made to northern France. One of these became the first 'Circus'. In the hope that the German fighters would react more intensively to our fighter penetrations into their territory, a Circus consisted of a squadron or wing of bombers, originally Blenheims, heavily escorted by several wings of fighters. To encourage enemy response, sensitive targets such as enemy airfields, ports and railway marshalling yards were selected. The conception of these operations closely resembled the *Luftwaffe*'s fast-running Ju 88 raids with their large escorts in the final stages of the Battle of Britain. The objectives were the same, that is to decimate the opposing fighter strength.

Accordingly, number one Circus was launched on 10th January 1941. It was of modest proportions consisting of nine Blenheims, escorted by three wings of Hurricanes and Spitfires, targeted on a German ammunition dump just inland of Calais. The three squadrons of the Biggin Hill wing led by Sailor Malan provided the withdrawal cover. It was a singulariy uneventful operation as little enemy reaction was seen. It was, however, the prologue to much hectic air fighting which was to occupy Fighter Command for the next three years.

The night blitz on London was increasing and desperate efforts were mounted to try and stem up the tide. Day fighters were despairingly despatched to patrol areas in the path of the inbound bomber stream, but without airborne radar which had not yet been perfected, or the occasional searchlight illumination it was like looking for a needle in a haystack. We could see the blazing fires in London being continually stoked up, but sighting the bombers responsible was well nigh impossible. I once saw the glow of engine exhausts passing beneath me but when I turned to follow, they melted into the blackness.

In the following month the weather brightened up and high level sweeps to north-west France were under way. In the course of these I had a salutary lesson that it doesn't pay to get too smart. We met some 109's in mid-Channel where all aircraft were pulling long dense contrails across the sky. As we neared one enemy *Schwarm*, the formation wheeled and headed back south with us in pursuit. I slowly overtook a 109 which was well out of range and I fondly imagined he was unlikely to see me if I hid in his contrail. After popping up a couple of times to assess my closing rate, I suddenly realised that maybe this tactic wasn't so clever and that two could play the same game. Sure enough I sighted another 109 behind me following my contrail and he was a lot closer to me than I was to his mate. My clever ruse was about to prove disastrous. I forgot the first target and broke around as hard as possible to get after the second one, but the turning circle was too great and I could only loose off a hopeful squirt as he faded from range.

A few weeks later 66 was moved to Exeter. We were very sorry to leave the activity and camaradie of Biggin Hill only to be dumped into a relatively inactive west country area. Our forebodings proved right and we once more launched into the soul-destroying monotony of eternal convoy patrols. No doubt they were vitally necessary from the Navy's point of view, but for us they were boring in the extreme. Fortunately there was a welcome break in the routine when we moved up to Tangmere for a Circus to Cherbourg docks. Taking along six Blenheims, six squadrons of Spitfires headed off for the target. The expected Luftwaffe fighter activation did not materialize, but the operation proved invaluable in revealing a number of problems involving the operation of over seventy Spitfires in one entity.

Back to normal in the rustic west country environment, 66 was moved even further west to Perranporth in Cornwall. This was about as far afield as one can get in the UK without an aircraft carrier. Strictly on our own without any other squadrons to help out, we intensified our shepherding of the ponderous convoys into the Channel. Concluding one of these irksome missions one day I landed back at the airfield with my wheels retracted. In 500-hours of flying Spitfires, I had never before come close to such horrendous negligence. Suffice to say that, although my Spitfire was only slightly damaged and after repair was flying again in a few days, I was deemed tour-expired and posted for a period off operations.

Accordingly my posting came through to No 59 Operational Training Unit (OTU) as an instructor on Hurricanes. Although sad to leave 66 after two and a half eventful years, I was not sorry to leave the god-forsaken wartime county of Cornwall. Arriving at the OTU's location of Crosby-on-Eden near Carlisle, my slightly resentful attitude of being posted from the squadron evaporated somewhat when I found a number of others of my vintage already there. Pete Illingworth, Fanny Orton, Peter Dunning-White and myself commanded the four flights and Denis David did his best to co-ordinate our activities.

The pupils to be trained as fighter pilots were arriving in droves from the training establishments in Canada. They were extremely keen but very raw and low on flying time. We gave each one a couple of rides in the Miles Master dual trainers before letting them loose in a Hurricane. To us inexperienced instructors, some of these checks took years off our lives; we couldn't believe there were so many hairy techniques in getting an aircraft aloft and down again. Pressure of time however wouldn't allow us to dally around giving basic instruction. Whenever a pupil displayed some ability, we strapped him to a Hurricane and stood back to pray for the best. The results were spectacular. Hurricanes staggered into the sky and, after a suitable pause 'gaining air experience', returned to attempt the landing. They attacked the runway from all angles; some held off much too high and flat-stalled with sickening thumps on to squared tyres, some swung off the landing area in a series of heart-stopping ground loops hopefully staying inside the airfield, and others belted in far too fast in a succession of kangaroo bounds until brought to rest by the mud off the end of the strip – sometimes standing vertically on the propeller. Still, there were remarkably few casualties, and the events spoke volumes for the rugged construction of the Hawker Hurricane.

Having survived the first week of the course, the kids began to come to terms with the Hurricane. We could then get down to imparting the knowledge required of a squadron fighter pilot. All the basics such as battle formations, recommended attacks, gunnery and so on were drilled home plus Sailor's Ten Rules. Towards the end of the course when the students had a fair idea of what went on we tried to instil the current fighter tactic's with realislic mock combats.

On 22nd June 1941, Hitler broke the non-aggression pact with Stalin and launclied his armies eastwards. Fresh from flexing its muscles in the invasion of Finland the previous year, the Red Army had to back off under the weight of the German attack. After fighting alone for over a year Britain and the Commonwealth at last had an ally, however fickle this partner might be. Our older generations were dubious. They recalled the betrayal by Russia when she surrendered her arms in 1917, which not only prolonged World War I, but cost the lives of thousands of Allied servicemen.

In the first weeks of the German advance the *Luftwaffe* made mincemeat of the Red Air Force. German fighter ace Oberstleutnant Heinz Bär summed up the contempt of the *Luftwaffe* for the Russian pilots and aircraft when he commented, 'Their tactics consisted of flying along reading the *Red Star Weekly*.' The fantastic losses of the Red Air Force led to a demand by Russia on Britain for help. Despite the RAF's shortage of fighters the government agreed to send a continuing supply of Hurricanes to fill the need. With the object of teaching the Russians to fly and maintain these aircraft, No 151 wing, consisting of two Hurricane squadrons was formed and despatched to Archangel. At our lowly OTU level several pilots were destined to Join this task force.

We instructors were told that we would be unlikely to return to operational squadrons in less than a year. This was distressing to contemplate and in an effort to beat the system, I volunteered for transfer to the Merchant Shipping Fighter Unit (MSFU). This outfit was the result of desperate measures to provide more air protection to the merchant ships of the Atlantic convoys. The menace arose from the German long-range aircraft, mostly Focke-Wulf Condors, whose reconnaissance missions were instrumental in concentrating the U-boat packs. Some merchant ships were modified to carry a catapult in order to launch a Hurricane to shoot down any enemy aircraft encountered in mid-Atlantic. It was very much a hit or miss affair. The unfortunate Hurricane pilots had nowhere to land back after their missions and had to bale out over the convoy, hopefully to be picked up by a friendly ship. There did not appear to be a great deal of future for ambitious pilots.

I flew to Speke for an interview and after hearing the requirements for the Job, I was most relieved to be told that I didn't qualify. Apparently flight lieutenants ranked too high and only pilot officers and flying officers were 'expendable' – in that order. One of these was Durex Kendal, my old colleague from 66. After a series of non-eventful Atlantic crossings, this gutsy officer finally shot into action over a supply convoy to Russia. He made the most of his opportunity and clobbered two Ju 88's before baling out into icy Arctic waters near an escorting destroyer. Sadly his parachute streamed and, although he was alive when picked up, he later died aboard.

Back at Crosby the next course we had to get operational was all Canadian. These boys were excellent material, and in my flight there were two characters in particular whom I was later delighted to see go on to become outstanding fighter pilots. They were George Keefer and Wally Conrad. Both became wing leaders, George being awarded a double DSO plus double DFC, and Wally collecting a DFC and bar. Between them they shot down twenty enemy aircraft over the Western Desert and Europe.

After four courses of instructing would-be fighter pilots the novelty began to pall, and it was time to try and get back to a squadron. Later in the summer I wrote a desperate plea to Billy Burton, my flight commander of Duxford days. Billy was then leading 616 Squadron at Westhampnett in the

Tangmere wing. He wrote back saying he would try to get me back to 11 Group and a few days later I received posting orders to, of all units, 616 Squadron.

There was a proviso in my orders which directed that en route for Westhampnett I was to report for interview with Group Captain (Ops) at HQ 11 Group at Uxbridge. The incumbent of this office was Group Captain Victor Beamish DSO, DFC the Irish rugger international who had made a personal impact on the *Luftwaffe* in the previous year's hostilities. With the build one would expect of a top class second row forward he was an inspirational leader to all the pilots in the Group. It was said that he knew every pilot by name which, with twenty-three squadrons to call on, was no mean feat. Rumour had it that he'd been a fighter pilot so long that he led the top cover on the Ascension.

Victor didn't mess around. He welcomed me back to the Group, looked at his watch and commented that he didn't think I'd have the time to catch the afternoon show scheduled for take-off at two o'clock. Since it was by then 12 noon and Uxbridge was some fifty-five miles from Tangmere, I didn't think so either.

No 616 was a fine squadron. With Billy Burton, the 1936 Cranwell Sword of Honour graduate at the helm, it couldn't be otherwise. My appointment was to fill the vacancy of flight commander B flight. None other than Johnnie Johnson held the reins in A flight. Johnnie exemplified the British bulldog type, fearless, uncompromising and tough. He learnt his trade in the demanding school of Douglas Bader's Duxford and Tangmere wings, often as a junior officer flying wingman to the maestro. When I joined 616, Johnnie was by then well launched on his fabulous career in which he would end the war as the top scoring Allied fighter pilot in the European theatre with thirty-eight kills. Significantly, all his victims were *Luftwaffe* single-engined fighters, the most formidable opponents to vanquish.

My stay with 616 was destined to be short-lived. Only a week later Victor Beamish flew into Westhampnett and went into a huddle with Billy Burton. Victor then took me aside and explained that 616 was being moved north for a rest from operations. He wanted to know if I would like to stay with the squadron or remain in 11 Group. Since I'd hardly had a chance to get to know the chaps and that I'd hibernated for four months at an OTU, I plumped for 11 Group. This seemed to be the right answer and Victor told me to swap places with Roy Marples who was then tour-expired in 41 Squadron. Roy had flown for a very long period of operations dating back to the outbreak of war and had thoroughly earned his break. Victor Beamish's personal touch in keeping an eye on all his pilots thereby retaining the Group at maximum efficiency was typical of this charming, yet very tough Irishman. I packed my bags and moved the few miles down the road to 41 Squadron's habitat at Merston.

The Tangmere squadrons were still keenly feeling the loss of their illustrious wing leader Douglas Bader. A few weeks earlier he had collided with a 109 in a a scrap over France. How he managed to bale out of a Spitfire with the handicap of two tin legs was a mystery, but nothing was impossible with that determined character. He was taken prisoner by the Germans, and we lost his aggressive and brilliant leadership for the rest of the war.

When the weather was good we continued the sweeps over northern France keeping the *Luftwaffe* pilots pinned back over their own territory,. When conditions worsened we kept up the pressure with low level operations termed 'Rhubarbs' in formations of two or four aircraft looking for targets of opportunity. We were now equipped with the Spitfire Mark Vb which carried the weightier punch of two 20-mm cannons in its armament and made the strafing of railway locomotives, river barges and shipping that more effective.

The 7th December, 1941, brought the news of Pearl Harbour. A shocked American nation responded with an immediate declaration of war on Japan. Intoxicated by the Nipponese audacity, Hitler dragged his lackey Mussolini into a state of hostilities against the United States within days. Unfortunate as this all was for America, British morale was considerably boosted that we now had a steadfast ally. Victory was no longer in doubt; it was just a matter of time before the vast American resources in men and materials could be brought to bear. 'The Yanks are coming', drooled the song. We hoped they wouldn't hang about.

Later in the year, we lost our squadron commander, Elmer Gaunce, a likable Canadian who got bounced in a scrap with some 109's near Dieppe;

unfortunately he lost his life in the action. His place was filled by an extremely press-on South African, Piet Hugo. He arrived with a formidable record in which during the previous year he had left a trail of devasted German fighters, bombers, seaplanes, ships, locos and anything else that moved into his gunsight. His marksmanship was superb and whenever he got near an enemy aircraft he was absolutely lethal. He would succinctly describe an accent in his picturesque Afrikaner accent as: 'The blody bastard knew what was blody coming, and he blody well got it!' Nobody ever queried it.

To celebrate Piet's arrival I promptly got the mumps, an ailliction with which I wondered what I'd done to deserve such a tate. As I finished my sick leave I received a telegram promoting me to command No 91 Squadron at Hawkinge.

CHAPTER EIGHT

'BACK, CHAPS, WE'RE IN THE SHIT'

Squadron Leader J J 'Chris' Le Roux, DFC

In the latter stages of the Battle of Britain, No 421 Fighter Flight was created whose mission was to provide 'spotter' patrols. The aim was to despatch singleton or pairs of fighters to pass sighting reports of enemy formations approaching and crossing the English coast. This ensured early contact with the enemy and the fighters broadcast running radio commentaries on the position, height, heading and other pertinent details on the incoming raids. These confirmed or otherwise the radar and Royal Observer Corps information, and in effect provided the controllers with eyes to appreciate the up to date situation.

Originally 421 Flight was armed with Hurricane Mark I's, but the hazardous nature of the missions in which a number were shot down very soon forced a re-equipment with the latest Spitfire Mark II's with all their advantage of superior height and speed. No 421 was commanded by Flight Lieutenant Paddy Green, a South African; he and his fellow pilots valiantly fulfilled the dangerous role and their efforts resulted in the most accurate interceptions by our fighter squadrons. Among the courageous originals were Paddy Barthropp, Billy Drake, Jas Storrar, 'Orange' O'Meara, Polly Perkins and two press-on flight sergeants, Don McKay and James Gillies. All were to considerably enhance their records as the war progressed and collect a load of well earned decorations.

As the *Luftwaffe*'s daylight bomber offensive faded out, the spotter role of 421 Flight diminished, but the individualistic nature of the unit was retained. There existed a paramount requirement for reconnaissance of the French and Belgian Channel ports to monitor the continual movement of German coastal shipping. Accordingly, 421 Flight was expanded to become No 91 Squadron. Stationed at Hawkinge near Folkestone, the squadron was less than fifteen minutes flying time from Cap Gris Nez and ideally situated to carry its specific sorties. 91 was part of the Biggin Hill Sector whose ops room provided control of all its activities.

The heavy responsibilities of the sector commander were borne by the much revered Group Captain Dicky Barwell, who flew with the wing whenever he could extract himself from his multifarious administrative duties. One day his engine cut dead on take-off, forcing him to crash land in a valley just beyond the runway where the impact was violent enough to break his vertebrae - but nothing so trivial as a broken back inhibited his zest for partaking in operations, and for several months he flew sorties with his body encased in plaster.

Having keyed up the Biggin Hill Wing to the most efficient fighting machine in the Command, Sailor Malan left for a well-deserved rest from operations. Jamie Rankin took over as wing leader and kept up the momentum. Blessed with superb eyesight, Jamie like Sailor was always fully aware of all that was going on among the squadrons he was leading. All the pilots knew that with Jamie in the lead they would never get jumped; attacked yes, but never bounced by an unseen enemy.

Such was the sky high morale of the Biggin Hill Sector when I took over 91. The squadron's *modus operandi* differed from other fighter units, and its reconnaissance background had earned it the tab of 'Jim Crow'.

Normally, the first and last sorties of each day were routine recces known as 'Milk runs' ranged along the French and Low Countries' coasts to check on overnight movements of enemy shipping. One run took in the ports from Calais to Flushing and the other between Boulogne and Le

Havre. To reduce the vulnerability of these singleton flights we had to depend on speed which we attained by climbing out across the Channel to around 17,000-feet and then, on setting course, trimming the aircraft into a slight dive at maximum cruising revs. There was no point in starting any higher as we needed to be below 14,000-feet over the ports, otherwise it made observation of details too difficult. We nipped across each port in turn taking a close look at the docks and noting the estimated size and numbers of ships present. With constant practice we knew the geography of each port by heart, and could tell instantly if there was any change. Normally the only opposition was flak, but slight changes in heading negated its accuracy. After checking the final port in the line we dived away some miles from the coast and returned to Hawkinge at sea level.

Weather recces followed a similar pattern, except that the runs started around 30,000-feet covering a large arc of occupied territory in a fast descending curve. Essential details embracing cloud levels, coverage, visibility and precipitation were accurately recorded over a wide area.

Air-sea rescue operations figured largely in our functions. Almost every morning some unfortunate crew struggling to bring a badly damaged bomber back to England from a previous night's raid over Germany would be forced to ditch in the oggin. Provided we had a reasonable bearing along which to mount the search, more often than not we found them floating in their dinghy. Once they were sighted the rescue operations cranked into action, and it was our responsibility to escort the Walrus amphibian aircraft and the high speed RAF launches to the scene. Likewise the tail end of fighter sweeps and circuses nearly always coughed up at least one Spitfire pilot whose aircraft had been sorely hit and who had managed to withdraw to the Channel before baling out. Such relatively unspectacular work kept us pretty busy. Sometimes, if the rescues were close to the French coast and the *Luftwaffe* attempted to intervene, there could be some hairy low-level action.

The pilots of 91 Squadron were a mixed representation of the Allied air forces. Two ex-Battle of Britain pilots commanded the flights, Frank Silk and New Zealander Bob Spurdle. Among the other characters were 'Diamond Jim' Brady from Canada and Sergeant Omdahl, an Australian. Two more pilots of British descent hailed from South America. They were a couple of the select few to wear the initials BLAV on their uniform, signifying an identity the Air Ministry whimsically described as 'British Latin American Volunteer'.

Tagging along with us most of the time was an extraordinary Frenchman who rejoiced under the nom de guerre of Moses Demozay. His real name was *Capitaine* Jean Morlaix, late of the *Armée de l'Air*, but he dropped this identity for fear of being branded a deserter when he escaped from occupied France in 1940.

He never smiled; with jet black hair and an equally black drooping moustache, he resembled an old world Mexican desperado. Moses decreed his own commandments; King's Regulations meant nothing to him. Adopting lone wolf tactics he never flew with anyone else if he could avoid it. His forte was to wage a one man war with the Luftwaffe, and it was quite remarkable how he successfully hunted down obliging targets to dump in the Channel.

Possessed of a Gallic, indeed Gaullic short fuse temperament he was inclined to explode into unpredictable exploits. On one memorable occasion he approached to land at Hawkinge, which was a large grass airfield without runways, and found his path obstructed by a tractor towing a gang mower. Bawling French obscenities over the R/T at Flying Control, he retracted his wheels and fired a short burst of machine gun fire some yards ahead of the tractor. The terrified driver lit for parts unknown while the tractor steered itself off the airfield. Only Moses could get away with that.

When I first clapped eyes on him my thoughts were in accord with the saying, 'I don't know about the enemy, but my God, he frightens me.' Having blazed a trail of strife as much among the Allies as the Axis, he survived the war only to be killed shortly afterwards in a flying accident near Paris.

Unknown to us the Joint Chiefs of Staff and other upper reaches of the hierarchy were preoccupied with the threat of a break-out from Brest of the German capital ships *Scharnhorst*, *Gneisenau* and *Prinz Eugen*. Numerous raids by Bomber Command in the previous months had failed to inflict enough damage on the ships to ensure their being kept bottled up in the port. Once free of the blockade, the carnage these powerful warships were capable of wreaking on our Atlantic supply convoys was incalculable.

The German intention to move the three heavy ships to a less vulnerable port was known to be imminent. Contingency plans were prepared to oppose any courses of action the ships might take when they reached the open sea. Once the break-out was under way the Navy and Air Force were to execute counter-action and the classified code to initiate the operations was 'Fuller'. Unfortunately, this vital piece of information got clogged in the chain and did not filter down to the fighter squadrons of 11 Group.

The early morning Milk runs of 12th February 1942 returned. The pilot on the Boulogne to Le Havre sortie reported that he had nothing to record as far as Dieppe, but that beyond that the weather clamped right down on the sea and he could penetrate no further. Shortly before ten o'clock I received a phone call from Squadron Leader Bill Igoe, the senior controller at Biggin Hill Operations, saying that there was considerable German fighter activity in the Somme estuary area. He was puzzled as to their intentions as they appeared to be staying in much the same position and had been there for some time. He thought it possible that they were giving cover to some sort of shipping and asked me to go and have a look but to be 'damned careful as there were a lot of Huns about.'

Heeding Bill's warning I selected Sergeant Beaumont as my No 2 and briefed him on the set-up. We flew along the cloud base which varied between about 1,200 and 1,800-feet. This gave us the opportunity to nip into cloud if we encountered too many German fighters. Following the coast past Le Touquet towards the Somme estuary we suddenly ran into some bursts of heavy flak. Banking into a turn we peered down through the rain and sighted a large oval of destroyers and smaller escorts in the middle of which were three much larger ships in line astern; all were leaving creamy wakes indicting that the force was moving fast.

My first reaction that the Royal Navy was a bit off course was soon dispelled when we saw flak guns on the deck firing at us. Calling Beaumont to break off we climbed up to the cloud base again. As we turned across the flotilla we spotted two fighters beneath the cloud, but because of rain on our windscreens we could not immediately identify them. We closed to about 500-yards on their tails and then I saw they were Spitfires. Calling Beaumont to break off we climbed up to the cloud base again. As we did so, we saw the two Spitfires dive down and open up with cannon on some E-boats in the outer convoy screen. It was obviously imperative that we should get this disturbing information back to Hawkinge and as we set course we eyeballed a big gaggle of German fighters over the French coast which hastened our decision.

There existed a regulation stating that strict radio silence must be maintained in matters concerning reconnaissance intelligence. Not being informed of the code-word 'Fuller' and its significance, I decided to break the rule and called in the clear to Bill Igoe at Biggin Hill Ops reporting what we had seen.

I was still not sure of the identity of the big ships, but after we landed Sergeant Beaumont was convinced that one of them was the *Scharnhorst*. Before becoming a pilot he had served in the RAF Marine Section at Gosport and had seen the *Scharnhorst* at a pre-war Naval review. When I telephoned my report Bill Igoe listened in and cranked me straight through to the incredulous 11 Group controller. Unfortunately the AOC, Sir Trafford Leigh-Mallory, was away at Northolt and I got nowhere in conveying the seriousness of the situation. Thirty minutes later the two Spitfires which Beaumont and I had seen over the German convoy landed at Kenley. The pilots were Victor Beamish, who by then was the Station Commander, and the Wing Leader, Finlay Boyd. They had maintained R/T silence and, since they hadn't called it, were as ignorant of 'Fuller' as we were. But their report married up with ours; obviously the representations of a Group Captain and a Wing Commander carried more weight than those of a Squadron Leader and Sergeant Pilot.

After an interminable and inexcusable delay the various Commands were alerted and the response ground into action. By then it was almost too late as the *Scharnhorst* and her cohorts were off Dover and steaming at over thirty knots into the North Sea. The British sea and air blockade had been well and truly penetrated; moreover, the inclement weather rendered powerful counter action impotent. The Navy had no sizeable warships based in the Channel area capable of lethal engagement, and because of the low cloud coverage. Bomber Command squadrons were unable to attack using their armour-piercing bombs which were ineffective if dropped from lower than 7,000-feet. Nothing could detract from the courageous but unavailing efforts of the smaller units to stop the rot. Some uncoordinated torpedo drops were made by a few Beauforts of Coastal Command and the Naval Motor Torpedo Boats, but none was successful.

The action climaxed with a desperate torpedo attack by six antiquated Swordfish aircraft of the Fleet Air Arm led by Lieutenant-Commander Esmonde. Five of these old 'Stringbags' were shot out of the sky by the lethal flak from the German fleet before they got into release range, and the sixth was hacked down by a covering 109. For this gallant action against all odds Esmonde was awarded a posthumous Victoria Cross.

Conversely, however, the German staffs were justifiably mystified at the slowness of British reaction just when they expected a spate of murderous opposition. *General* Adolph Galland, the *Luftwaffe* fighter ace who was responsible for the protective air cover during the escape bid described the tension at his headquarters. I am indebted to him for permission to quote from his absorbing book *The First and the Last*.

> At 10 o'clock British time an alerting radio message from a British fighter was intercepted by our listening service. It said nothing except that a large German naval formation consisting of three capital ships and about twenty warships was steaming at high speed towards the Straits of Dover, present position about fifteen miles off the mouth of the Somme. The secret was out.
>
> At last we had to accept this as a fact according to the intercepted radio message. The decision to drop all attempts at disguising our operation lay with me. The fact that the first counter measures by the British Command were not taken for another hour proved the wisdom of my decision not to be driven to rash measures by this alarming message, but to continue to observe the precautions intended to keep the operation hidden from the enemy. The British give 11.05 British time as the time of the discovery, yet the first report of the British fighter was a whole hour earlier. It appears they gave no credence to the report; they simply sent up another reconnaissance plane and ordered a full alert. An hour later the second aircraft brought confirmation of the report, which had been regarded as impossible. Churchill states that the British Admiralty did not receive this information before 11.25.

General Galland's reference to the delay in reaction after my R/T call to Bill Igoe are roughly correct. It took Beaumont and myself all of fifteen minutes to land back at Hawkinge and make our report. Beamish and Boyd took a further half hour in their longer flight to Kenley, and then Leigh-Mallory had to be recalled from Northolt to Uxbridge before any decisive action was taken.

Despite the unsuccessful attempts of our defensive forces to halt the Channel dash, the German ships did not escape unscathed. Minefields previously laid by Bomber Command along the likely escape route impeded the escape through the North Sea. At 2.30pm, the *Scharnhorst* struck a magnetic mine which inflicted enough damage to arrest her progress. Hasty temporary repairs enabled her to proceed, and she picked up sufficient speed to retain contact with the main body of escorting warships. After dark that evening the *Gneisenau* struck another air-laid mine, but although her speed was reduced she was able to continue her progress to her destination on the Elbe. Shortly afterwards the *Scharnhorst* sustained substantial damage when she struck yet another mine and stopped for nearly an hour. Seriously impaired, and with over 1,000 tons of water shipped aboard, she finally limped into Wilhelmshaven to join her cohorts.

Nevertheless, the Channel Dash was a daring and superbly executed operation by the Germans, albeit somewhat fortunately aided by the inclement weather. Their audacious success in the face of formidable Royal Navy and RAF forces created a public furore. A furious Prime Minister Churchill ordered an immediate enquiry to which Beaumont and I were summoned to give evidence among a host of heavily braided witnesses. The dust took a long time to settle, if it ever did.

The Messerschmitt which the *Luftwaffe* had used exclusively as the standard single seat fighter had been beefed up in performance with modifications to engine and airframe. The later model was introduced to combat in 1941 and designated the Me 109F. To counter it we had the Spitfire Mark VB which was fitted with the more powerful Rolls Royce Merlin Mark XXV and was provided with a greater punch to the armament by the substitution of two Hispano belt fed 20-mm cannon in place of four of the original eight .303 in Brownings. Early in 1942, however, the enemy upstaged us with the introduction of a formidable opponent in the Focke-Wulf 190. This radial engined single seat fighter carried a heavy calibre armament, and was much faster than the Spitfire Mark V at all altitudes.

Such was the order of battle for the opposing sides in the spring of 1942. RAF fighters were at a performance disadvantage, yet the pressure to keep the *Luftwaffe* at bay over its own territory had to be sustained in order to tie down large numbers of enemy fighters which could otherwise be released for use on the Russian front. The sweeps and circuses continued even though our casualties mounted to two to one against us. Most of our pilots who baled out in the combats were captured and were not recoverable, yet the loss rate was considered acceptable as the training machine was by then up to replacement capacity.

One March afternoon the alarm bells at 11 Group sounded. Victor Beamish was missing. He had been out with the Kenley wing over Abbeville enticing the Focke-Wulf boys to come up and play on their own doorstep. The wing got embroiled in a fighting withdrawal over the Somme estuary and the action was so hectic that nobody saw what happened to him. 91 laid on the usual air sea rescue search augmented by the Kenley squadrons who flew out in relays to the area. The quest continued unsuccessfully until dusk and was reactivated at first light the next day. If Victor had managed to bale out and take to his dinghy we should have found him, but there was no sign. The only hope was that he could have come down over France and be taken prisoner of war. Unfortunately this did not transpire and we lost yet another brave and inspirational leader.

Stung into retaliation by our relentless offensive, the *Luftwaffe* resorted to sneak raids on our south coast towns and ports. Small formations of fighter bombers flew in fast at low level pulling up at the last moment to drop their bombs indiscriminately on so called targets. Our radars were unable to pick them up until a very late stage as their approaches were below the horizon line of sight. In most cases insufficient time was available to provide interceptions by our own fighters either from standing patrols or stand-by states. Those engagements which did take place were usually fortuitous in that our defending fighters happened to be in the area at the time.

In the Biggin Hill sector these raids concerned 91 Squadron more than others because of our disposition on the south coast. Despite this, our success in intercepting the raids was practically nil and caused us much frustration. I flew up to Biggin Hill and took my worries to the sector commander. Dicky Barwell was as concerned as I was and we had a long discussion with the senior controller, Bill Igoe. Ultimately Dicky suggested that with Bill controlling he would accompany me on a standing patrol the same evening to try and assess first-hand what the problems were.

We took off from Biggin Hill an hour before sunset and patrolled just off the coast between Dungeness and Beachy Head. There was a very thick haze up to 16,000-feet and we stationed just above it. As we approached Beachy, Bill warned us of unidentified plots in our vicinity and we peered into the haze for signs of activity. Suddenly I sighted two fighters approaching us out of the glare of the setting sun and gave a warning to Dicky who was abreast of me and nearer to them. The leading fighter, which flew close over the top of me, I identified as a Spitfire and called the fact to Dicky. I watched it as it faded to my rear and then turned back to see the second aircraft, another Spit, behind Dicky and already opening fire on him.

Calling an urgent break to Dicky I flew on a collision course at his attacker and succeeded in distracting him enough to force a break-away. I turned back close over the top of Dicky, whose aircraft was flaming from the petrol tank, and I could see him desperately trying to open the canopy to bale out. I glanced back to see the first Spit swinging in behind me and opening fire. I broke hard round and down into the haze to shake him off, but search as I might I could see no sign of Dicky. My frantic calls to him bore no response and I circled down through the murk to the Channel. All I could find was what I took to be an oil slick on the surface, but there was no sign of either a parachute or a dinghy.

I flew despondently back to Biggin to report the tragedy. Despite intensive air sea rescue searches, no trace of Dicky was ever found. I felt awful about it and somehow responsible for losing a gallant officer. No blame could be apportioned to Bill Igoe's control organisation; they did their job. It is significant, however, that the subsequent Court of Inquiry revealed that the two Spitfires which caused the calamity came from an Allied squadron in the Tangmere sector and that, incredibly, one pilot was on his first operational sortie and the leader on his second.

So died a superb commander in most deplorable circumstances. With his body still strapped in plaster to protect his cracked vertebrae, Dicky probably found it too severe a handicap either to abandon his aircraft or even to jettison the canopy. But being the man he was he would have been the first to forgive the trigger-happy Tangmere pilots who, itching to claim their first Hun, couldn't tell the difference between a Messerschmitt and a Spitfire.

Jim Crow's black plumage was going grey. The movement of hostile ships around the Channel ports decreased and little cognisance was taken of any of the squadron's reports. Even the sighting of the German capital ships, possibly the most urgent single item of naval intelligence supplied in the war, had been treated with scepticism. As a reconnaissance squadron, 91 was shovelling smoke. It was time to move on.

CHAPTER NINE

'LET'S FACE IT'

Wing Commander Jamie Rankin DSO, DFC

At Biggin Hill, Jamie Rankin had for some time been seeking permission to try out a new offensive tactic with the wing. Previously the sweeps had involved the squadrons bound for France to climb out gaining combat altitude from take-off. On a Circus this was essential in order that our escorting fighters could be correctly stationed over the bombers before crossing the French coast, but it meant that as soon as the formations attained a few thousand feet all aircraft were picked up by the opposing radar. Consequently the enemy had time to assess the raid's strength, direction and height and could at leisure concentrate his fighters in their most advantageous positions to intercept.

Jamie's theory was that using an entire wing on a pure sweep without bombers we could approach the hostile coast at low level below the radar pick-up height. He calculated that once the wing entered the line of sight range a few miles from the French coast, a swift climb should provide enough height to arrive over the *Luftwaffe* airfields before their fighters had enough warning to be fully organised. 11 Group agreed to give the ruse a try and an operation was scheduled for 5th June with the German fighter airfield complex at Abbeville as the objective. Anxious to take part in this venture I flew to Biggin and poor-mouthed Jamb into slotting me in as his wingman.

Jamie briefed the wing on the mission. He concluded: 'I'm certain there are often more Huns beneath us which we don't see because we're over concentrating on blocking the bounce from above – Let's face it, if we give them minimum warning, we should catch them coming up!'

The wing stacked on the runway and at the zero minute took off in flights of four only seconds apart. I glued on to Jamie's right wing as he unstuck and swung into a gentle left-hand turn to settle down on course. Observing strict radio silence, the wing's three squadrons belted south east across Kent with everyone below 100-feet. We contour-chased down the valleys in an exhilarating ride to Dungeness where Jamie altered course slightly and headed for the Somme estuary. The wing looked an inspiring sight as thirty-six Spitfires squatted over the Channel, building up the speed to maximum cruise. A few minutes later the French coast shimmered out of the haze as Jamie leading 133 (Eagle) Squadron took us upstairs in a high speed climb which penetrated the enemy radar coverage. Settling around 15,000-feet we bored in towards our target.

Brian Kingcome took 72 Squadron a couple of thousand feet above the wing leader as Myles Duke-Woolley swept 124 Squadron up to the top cover station. Some inaccurate flak trailed behind us. It didn't bother us but it was indicative that the enemy was fully aware of our presence. Moreover, the bursts betrayed our position to any hawk-eyed *Luftwaffe* fighters who might be in the area. Sure enough, as we turned over Abbeville, a gaggle of Me 109's fell on us out of the sun but not before we saw them. 124 Squadron turned into them and engaged as 72 Squadron cut across to help. At the same time Jamie winged over calling a sighting beneath us. As I followed him down I saw a string of Focke-Wulf 190's climbing up in one's and two's, and way below more pairs taking off from an airfield. Jamie snaked down behind a 190 and let fly from close range; a cluster of shells from his cannons flashed into the fuselage around the cockpit area. Flame and smoke shot back as his victim fell into its fatal dive. Without pause Jamie moved over and belted another 190 as it struggled for altitude. Pieces of cowling and the canopy peeled off, followed by the pilot who hastily departed in his parachute. Lost in admiration at this awesome display of shooting I almost forgot my primary duty to guard our tails, but we were clear. Jamie called a reform of the excited American Eaglets and swung round back to where 72 and 124 were milling in their action. As we clawed back some height two Fw 190's flew in loose astern formation in front of us. Jamie fired deflection and seemed to get some strikes on each in turn as they swept past, but their speed took them out of range as they disappeared behind.

We rejoined the other two squadrons as they warded off the now spasmodic attacks from the split-up German fighters. Jamie ordered, 'Everybody out'. Noses down and tails up we roared through the coastal flak and out to the safety of the Channel. When we debriefed back at Biggin morale was sky high since there were no casualties and each squadron had a number of viable claims. Despite the fact that we had run into the Me 109's en route to the target, it was established that these boyos were airborne before we crossed in. The operation nevertheless was deemed an unqualified success. Jamie was elated. 'Let's face it,' he said, 'we can do that again!' For this action he was credited with a Fw 190 destroyed, a probable and two damaged. I ruefully contemplated the essential role of a fighter wing-man; I hadn't even fired my guns' A month later Brian Kingcome was promoted to take over the Kenley wing. I was lucky enough to be plucked from Hawkinge to take his place as CO of 72 Squadron. As a measure of his status as a leader, he handed over to me what surely ranked as the best drilled, most experienced and aggressive fighter squadron in the RAF. Brian introduced me to this cosmopolitan bunch of tough operators. Comprising the pilot complement about half were British together with two Australians, a Canadian, a New Zealander, a South African, two Americans and two Norwegians. 'A' flight was commanded by Canadian 'Timber' Woods and Aussie Hugo Armstrong led B flight. The squadron had just been rearmed with the Spitfire Mark IX, arguably the best fighter of the Supermarine string. Powered by a Rolls Royce Merlin Mark 61 engine, it incorporated a two stage supercharger which provided superior performance over any contemporary Luftwaffe fighter. 72 were delighted and viewed the future with boundless confidence.

I was soon to witness the mettle of this outfit. We swung straight into action with a series of sweeps and circuses over Northern France. On 26 July, we ran into a pack of Focke-Wulf 190's over St Omer and fought a running battle out of France toward Calais. Hugo's flight was being harried and got behind a bit. As we turned to help him out I got a fleeting shot at a 190 which attacked me head-on, but I couldn't pull enough deflection and fired beneath it. As it flashed over my canopy, Jack Kitchen behind me fastened on to it and blew it up. We got stuck into Hugo's mill as a 190 came streaking out of the fight underneath, which put it nicely in range for me to dive and belt it. Hits struck around the cockpit and wing roots as it flicked over and spun out. Meantime the mix-up resulted in several 190's being damaged while Hugo topped the lot by despatching another on fire.

It was great to be back at 'The Bump'. Hugo's victim turned out to be the 900th enemy aircraft destroyed by the Biggin Hill sector since the war started. To celebrate this unique milestone we repaired in the evening to Biggin's premier local, the White Hart at Brasted, where our matchless hostess Kath Preston laid on her usual instant party.

But this life of bliss was not to last. A week later the squadron was ordered north and coincidentally an even worse blow was the loss of five of our senior pilots all of whom were promoted and posted to other squadrons. Hugo took over 611, and Collie Mansfeld went with him. Timber Woods was designated CO of the renowned 249 Squadron in Malta and the two Jacks, Ratten and Kitchen, moved to Hornchurch. The final straw was having to hand over our brand-new Spit Mark IX's to our replacement Canadian Squadron, No 401, who in return saddled us with their clapped-out Mark Vs.

Our destination in 13 Group was a sparse wartime airfield at Morpeth in Northumberland. The sight of this hutted habitat was depressing, but we reckoned without the local citizens. Back in 1940 at the height of the Battle of Britain the *Luftwaffe* mounted a double-headed 'back-door' raid toward Northumberland and Yorkshire. The object was to ascertain what fighter reserves, if any, Fighter Command had which were not committed to the hectic fighting down south. Since the enemy bombers were launched from northerly bases in Norway and Denmark, the only fighter protection with sufficient range to undertake the operation were the twin-engined

Messerschmitt 110's. The first assault comprising over seventy Heinkel 111's and escorting Me 110's headed towards Newcastle and Sunderland. The supporting raid of fifty unescorted Ju 88's bore in on Hull. Both formations had a rough reception from six squadrons of Hurricanes and Spitfires, among which 72 Squadron based on Acklington was the first to intercept. As mentioned previously, the Me 110's were no match for the RAF's single seat fighters and the ensuing conflicts rapidly separated the bombers from their escorts. The raids were stricken to the extent of losing over a third of their numbers, and enemy aircraft were splattered down the coast from the Tyne to the Humber.

The Geordies of Northumberland never forgot the spectacle, and once their smoke signals established that 72 was again in their midst, the squadron was overwhelmed with invitations to social events of all kinds. Two years had elapsed since the 'back-door' debacle in which none of the current pilots had taken part. No matter, the squadron was the hero, and the generous citizens of Ashington and Morpeth laid on the hospitality despite the wartime rations and black market. All ranks in the squadron soon discovered that Geordie girls were excellent dancers, and that Newcastle Brown Ale had lost none of its pre-war potency!

Shortly afterwards the squadron moved to the airfield on Ayr racecourse where we were told to prepare for overseas deployment. Much had to be done as the unit expanded to become self-sufficient in transport, tentage, field kitchens, medical facilities and airfield defence. In a short time the complement increased to over 200 personnel. Not least we urgently needed to replace our recently posted officers. Pilots who had completed a tour of operations were largely in instructional roles with Operational Training Units or Flying Training Command, and these organisations were loath to part with such experience. Nonetheless, I submitted a list of names to a sympathetic AOC 13 Group, AVM Jock Andrews, who somehow overcame all obstacles. Shortly afterwards half a dozen old sweats emerged from their hibernant locations all over the Air Force and checked in to 72 Squadron for their second tour of operations. Among this hairy collection were Chas Charnock, Jimmy Corbin, Pete Fowler, Alan Gear, J Le Cheminant and D J Prytherch.

In the meantime, I had to report urgently to the AOC. Without going into detail he informed me that 13 Group was required to reinforce 11 Group for an important operation to be mounted in the near future. Well aware that 72 Squadron was depleted in mature pilots he informed me that 222, another of his squadrons based at Drem was in the same predicament. He had decided therefore that the two squadrons would temporarily pool their resources to form one unit with the most experienced pilots. 222 Squadron was to be the nominated outfit to proceed south.

Matters were further complicated in that a year before, 222's CO, Archie Winskill, had been shot down over France flying with Douglas Bader's Tangmere wing. He evaded capture by the Germans and returned to UK, but in view of his contacts with the French Resistance, the Air Ministry placed an embargo on him, forbidding him to fly over occupied France. Archie was a bit put out that he had to hand over his squadron to me at such a key time, and I sympathised with him entirely. Much embarrassment could have been avoided if his pilots had reinforced my squadron rather than vice versa.

In the event, on 16th August, I set course with eighteen Spitfires to deploy on Biggin Hill for the forthcoming 'operation'. There we had a couple of days to work up and we carried out some sweeps over France.

During the evening of 18th August, we were briefed on the operation code-named 'Jubilee'. This was the infamous raid on Dieppe scheduled for the following day in which the 2nd Canadian Division including tanks were to probe the strength of the German coastal defenses. The intention was that the assault should be of sufficient strength that, in order to counteract the likelihood of our Allied invasion, the enemy would be forced to retain large elements of his forces in North-West Europe. Inevitably this would reduce the pressure on the hard pressed Russians in the East. To provide air support for Jubilee the RAF assembled a powerful strike force of aircraft to neutralise important tactical targets together with a massive fighter umbrella.

Every airfield in the south of England was loaded with aircraft. Apart from a formidable force of tactical bombers, Hurricane fighter/bombers and a back-up of the American 97th Bomb Group flying B 17's, Fighter Command fielded a defensive air cover of no less than fifty-one fighter squadrons, mostly Spitfires. At Biggin Hill our newly formed wing consisted of 222, together with 602 Squadron commanded by Pete Brothers, and the recently operational American Air Corps 307th (Spitfire) Squadron led by Major Marvin McNickle.

At the ungodly time of 3am we reported our readiness state and awaited our turn to head for Dieppe. The night was dark but clear and as the fitters shut down their engine warm ups an eerie silence settled on the airfield. An hour later the quiet was shattered by the noise of Merlin engines as 111 Squadron took off from Kenley, a few-miles to the west of us. We watched the unusual sight of a dozen sets of navigation lights circling the base to form up and disappear to the south. Soon after dawn Pete Brothers fired up 602 and with a reverberating roar twelve Spitfires climbed away into the lightening sky. The air coverage shuttle service for the beaches was under way.

Our turn came at six o'clock. Eric 'Tommy' Thomas, the Biggin Hill wing leader who had recently taken over from Jamie Rankin, elected to fly with us in 222. We took off accompanied by the American 307th 'Pursuit'. Slotting in to the air corridor from Beachy Head to Dieppe we settled down at our unbelievably low assigned altitude between 4,000 and 8,000-feet; a tactical handicap I complained to Tommy about before we took off. He shrugged his shoulders and agreed with me but opined that 'orders are orders and we'd better get on with it'.

Approaching the French coast we were greeted by an incredible spectacle. Ships of all sizes ploughed around the Channel within a few miles of the beaches. Navy warships blasted off intermittent broadsides at inland targets, whilst around the harbour and beyond brilliant flashes and explosions erupted in every direction. Great palls of smoke drifted away with the wind, and at all heights in the restricted area squadrons of Spitfires swung up and down their allotted patrol lines.

We moved into position and relieved the Tangmere wing which Johnny Walker took home to refuel. The 30-minute patrol time from our point of view was uneventful. We could see other squadrons higher above us getting involved in odd skirmishes with Me 109's and Fw 190's, but as we feared our designated patrol altitude was too low down to be effective. We did not have the height to precipitate aggressive action and on the contrary seemed to offer ourselves as targets for a fast acting bounce. Indeed the point was proved when the 307th 'Pursuit', stationed on our flank, were soundly jumped by some hit-and-run 190's. As a result, Lieutenant Ed Tovrea became their first casualty landing in the battle area to be captured and put in the bag.

Returning to Biggin to refuel, we were scheduled for three further patrols during the day and on each of them our height was pegged around 6,000-feet. Presumably the intention was for us to cut off any low-flying German bomber attacks on our ships and if so the planning staffs committed a cardinal error in restricting our freedom of manoeuvre. We needed to be much wider on the flanks of the assault with an altitude of at least 10,000-feet which would give us the initiative to jump any speedy raiders below us. The top scoring ace of World War I, Mick Mannock, said in 1917: 'Always above, seldom at the same level, but never beneath.' This maxim we had found emphatically emphasised during the previous three years, and it was frustrating in the extreme to find it ignored at Dieppe.

Our contribution to the day's operations consisted of four missions which totalled six exhausting hours' flying. Throughout the period we had witnessed our higher flying squadrons battling it out above us, but from our low slung station we were unable to join in. Even though we were relegated to a disadvantageous beat, we certainly had a grandstand view of the bloody struggle beneath us. The Canadian tanks sank into the soft sand of the beaches and became immobile. They and their exposed infantry suffered dire casualties from withering German artillery and small arms fire which was strategically dug in along the cliffs. At one point a number of lifeboats were seen to row frantically away from a Royal Navy control ship which took on a reddish hue and finally blew up with a mighty explosion; when the flame and smoke finally cleared, there was absolutely nothing left.

As we turned for home at the end of our last patrol covering the withdrawal, I pondered the fact that although we had nothing to claim for our efforts, mercifully our hastily assembled squadron had not been chewed to bits. At that moment a Fw 190 hurtled down from the cumulus cloud above and made a high speed pass at Sergeant Vic Evans stationed on the flank. The 190 loosed a short burst and plunged on down in a parabola we hadn't a hope of cutting off. Evans managed to stagger with his damaged Spit to Hawkinge where he successfully crash-landed. Our day-long anxieties of being jumped in such a way had been justified. We landed back at Biggin and debriefed.

So ended the Dieppe fiasco. The first Allied combined operation had tempted fate and got a bloody nose for it. The Royal Navy lost several precious ships it could ill afford and many other craft were severely damaged. As the Canadian tanks were unable to surmount the beach obstacles they could not support their infantry. Despite all attempts to neutralise the German coastal batteries they were able to subject the invaders to ruthless fire throughout the assault; to such an extent that the timed withdrawal had to be brought forward by two hours. Of the 5,000 who so confidently raided the beaches that morning the Canadian necrology exceeded 3,000.

In maintaining aerial protection over the battle area Fighter Command largely succeeded in its primary objective of defending the military and naval forces from air attacks. However, the posture imposed on the umbrella by the restricted area to which it was confined severely limited freedom of action, and in the continuous clashes during the day surrendered the initiative to the German fighters. In the final count the RAF lost over 100 aircraft to the fiftyor so by the *Luftwaffe*.

When events returned to normal, there was much conjecture as to whether it had all been worthwhile. No concrete objective had been achieved, at the cost of appalling casualties. The hierarchy subsequently maintained that the experience gained at Dieppe would have invaluable application for the ultimate Normandy invasion two years later. Maybe, but what a terrible price to pay.

Next day I took 222 Squadron back to Drem and handed back to Archie Winskill his pilots and aircraft. Shortly afterwards Archie was able to shed the irksome and frustrating restrictions imposed on his operations over northern Europe. He took command of 232 Squadron in the Mediterranean and proceeded to wreak revenge with interest on the unfortunate *Luftwaffe*.

I rejoined 72 with my clement of pilots and the next two months passed in hectic preparations for overseas duty. Finally at Ellesmere Docks we embarked with our crated Spitfires aboard a decrepit merchant ship called the *Fort Maclaughlin*. Joining a large convoy we pointed out to the Atlantic, destination unknown.

CHAPTER TEN

'IT LOOKS A BIT DICEY'

Squadron Leader Mickey Rook, DFC

The pilots of all the embarked squadrons were divided into two parties each and separated into different ships. Such planning by our seniors disclosed a morbid but no doubt prudent assumption that we might not all wind up at our intended destination. Facilities aboard the *Fort Maclaughlin* were strictly basic. The centre hold had been converted into a dormitory containing a couple of dozen rough hewn wooden bunks. This windowless drifting dungeon was to be our home for the next seventeen anxious days. The ship's captain called for volunteers as look-outs for hostile submarines and the response was overwhelming. Visions of our bedroom below being the most obvious torpedo target for any marauding U-boat spurred us topsides in tight fitting Mae Wests. The gallant captain was barely able to set foot on his own bridge as a crowd of keen-eyed fighter pilots eyeballed the rolling oggin for tell tale signs of periscopes.

Our Spitfires were crated and lashed to the deck, there being no space below since all available holds were stuffed with highly volatile ammunition and cans of aviation petrol. The convoy comprised over fifty similarly loaded ships resembling so many floating bombs as we wallowed ponderously toward the Azores. Fortunately this extensive diversion successfully dodged the U-boat packs and we turned east to Gibraltar. As we thankfully disembarked the sight of the formidable Rock raised our morale no end. We bade farewell to the ship's crew and left them with our unbounded admiration for the sailors of the Merchant Navy whose dedication in maintaining supplies to the nation utterly disregarded the perilous threats to their defenceless ships.

Halfway through our apprehensive voyage from UK, a BBC broadcast disgorged the news that Montgomery had finally got off his arse at El Alamein and gone forth to challenge Rommel. Though we had not yet been told, it was obvious that our immediate future would in some form provide support for the 8th Army's desert battle. We were given no time to dwell on it for as soon as we hit the dockside, we were trundled off to the east side of the Rock and there confined to camp for 'security reasons'. This seemed irrelevant at the time because just across the frontier in Spain we could see in their little hut some German agents busily logging our every move with mounting curiosity.

Operation '*Torch*' was on. We were part of the Anglo-American invasion of Algeria in an all out offensive to join up with the 8th Army and kick the Axis out of Africa. Wing leaders, squadron and flight commanders assembled for briefing. The Air Officer Commanding Gibraltar explained the operation plans whereby the primary British objective was the capture of the port of Algiers some 500-miles east of Gib. Emphasising the importance of timing for the air support forces, he pointed out that the Royal Marine Commandos and their US equivalents, the American Rangers, had the task of seizing the major airfield at Maison Blanche. Little was known as to how the French Vichy forces would react, or indeed in what strength they would be found. He stressed that the Commandos had only six hours from the time of their assault in which to capture the airfield. It was by no means certain there would be a friendly reception for the first fighter squadron timed to arrive from Gib on the six-hour deadline and without sufficient fuel to divert elsewhere.

Such an absurdity tickled the imagination of Mickey Rook, the CO of

43 Squadron: 'Ho, ho, ho,' he chortled – it looks a bit dicey.'

'Yes, Rook,' agreed the AOC. 'The first squadron in will be 43!'

Mickey took this to heart, and being a veteran of the previous year's task force teaching the Soviets to fly Hurricanes, had been vastly impressed by the rigorous Russian defence of their airfields in a tactical environment. He saw no reason why an enemy, let alone the Vichy forces at Maison Blanche, would react any differently. In the pre-dawn gloom before 43's departure from the Rock, he was seen to mount his aircraft armed with a murderous array of knives and pistols stuffed into various parts of his flying gear. In the event the Commandos had captured the airfield by the time 43 arrived, and Mickey was not required to perform a defence unto death of his precious Hurricane.

All the fighter aircraft were rapidly unloaded from the ships, taken out of their crates and assembled three deep along Gib's airstrip. We drew flying equipment from stores and air tested our aircraft in the brilliant light of the Mediterranean, such a contrast with the comparative gloom of Europe. The task force squadrons departed in a steady stream for Africa and, on 16th November, 72 arrived at Maison Blanche. The place bulged with aircraft of all types and activity bordered on organised chaos. The fighter squadrons had a built in disadvantage since their ground crews were still in convoy somewhere in mid-Atlantic. We had limited assistance to each squadron from small groups of about a dozen RAF Servicing Commandos, whose efficiency was little impaired by the contents of their tool kits which appeared to be confined to a spanner and a screwdriver. Every pilot became his own crew chief and in the process many revealed hitherto unsuspected talent and ingenuity. Our back-up equipment was still with our troops on the high seas and accommodation was non-existent. At night we wrapped our weary limbs in a couple of blankets sleeping fully clothed on the concrete floor of a French Air Force hangar.

The *Luftwaffe* decided to come and see what all the fuss was about and added to the confusion by bombing the harbour. The raids were greeted with traditional naval hospitality as every ship within ten square miles let go with all available guns. The pyrotechnics surpassed any Guy Fawkes or 4th July spectacle.

We endured a day and night in the Maison Blanche madhouse before 72 was ordered a further 300-miles east to Bône. There to greet us was Piet Hugo, now the wing leader of 322 Wing. The *Luftwaffe* had reacted with enviable speed to the Allied invasion and poured fighter squadrons into Tunisia from Sicily and France. Piet and his squadrons had moved equally quickly through Djidjelli to Bône wreaking en route the familiar Hugo trail of Teutonic mayhem. No sooner had we refuelled than Piet led 81 Squadron and us in 72 on a sweep to the Tabarka area. As we climbed out of Bône we sighted a lone Ju 88 pushing his luck as he crossed our track. We poured on the coals in a race to get there first but Piet got the edge and bored in on a full quarter attack. His shooting was a sight to behold, as in one long burst his cannon shells raked the enemy from nose to tail. With a momentary fiery explosion, it disintegrated and fell in a shower of bits.

The rest of the trip was uneventful and we landed back at Bône, but not to any respite. The Allied occupancy of this little port was vital to the supply and reinforcement of the fast-moving British 1st Army, hell bent on the capture of Tunis. The *Luftwaffe* knew this only too well and mounted relentless attacks on Bône's harbour and airfield. We were frantically busy servicing the aircraft, digging slit trenches and scrambling for patrols. On one of these Pilot Officer Owen 'Andy' Hardy notched up 72's first kill with a spectacular bounce on a Me 109 which shed its propeller and crashed into a hillside.

We in 72 were a part of 324 Wing and our commander, Group Captain Ronnie Lees, decided it was time to assemble his widely dispersed Spitfire squadrons into a cohesive unit. The British 1st Parachute Battalion had secured the airfield at Souk el Arba and we moved in. Tony Bartley's 111 were already there, George Nelson-Edwards turned up with 93 from Djidjelli, Jackie Sing with 152 leapfrogged across from Maison Blanche via Bône, and 225 Reconnaissance Squadron completed the set-up with their Hurricanes. Since our ground troops with our equipment had not yet disembarked in Africa, we were hard-pressed for aircraft servicing and living conditions. Ronnie Lees managed to persuade the Foreign Legion at Souk to lend us some sorely needed tents and cooking equipment, whereupon some semblance of order emerged.

Refuelling the aircraft was an arduous chore as we poured in the petrol from four gallon tins. Oil was in short supply and had to be rationed to the thirstiest engines. The ex-Boy Scouts among us pitched the French bell tents on a ration of two per squadron. After nightfall accommodation was somewhat crowded as a dozen or more pilots lay down to try and sleep with feet to the centre and parachutes for pillows. We needn't have bothered because overhead the *Luftwaffe* kept a relay of singleton bombers which all night long scattered nasty little anti-personnel butterfly bombs among us. Obviously sleep was a luxury with which we would have to dispense. The alternative was to get on with the war.

German resistance to the British 1st Army stiffened up and advanced elements of the Guards Brigade had to dig in at the key town of Medjez el Bab. *Luftwaffe* strikes were hammering our soldiers and RAF fighter patrols were concentrated over the battle zone. Radar coverage was not yet available but the contested area was so limited it was hardly needed. Both sides concentrated on the Medjez front and fierce clashes ensued.

During the last patrol on our second stay at Souk, we in 72 sighted a German transport convoy on a road near Mateur. We swept down out of the setting sun and strafed the vehicles which all erupted in intense flames. After landing we surmised that the fierceness of the fires indicated petrol cargoes possibly for supply to an airfield. First thing next morning we returned to the same area and found an even bigger convoy of trucks. Again we gave them the treatment and after flaming up the whole convoy, I called off the squadron intending to return to base.

As the formation reformed, my No 2, Pryth Prytherch, flying astern of me called up saying he had oil on his windscreen and could he take up an echelon position so that he could see better?

I acknowledged, and as he came up beside me, he made the laconic comment: 'It's not my oil, boss, it's yours"

He could see oil streaming down my lower fuselage from the engine. Unknown to me some part of the oil system must have been hit by light flak. I checked my oil pressure and temperature gauges; the former read zero, and the latter was off the clock.

I eased back the throttle and moved the prop pitch to fully coarse. Heading for the nearest point of the British lines the engine got steadily rougher but kept going for several minutes which spoke volumes for Rolls Royce reliability. Finally the works seized up and the prop clanked to a stop. Trimming into a gliding speed I kept heading west praying that I would reach friendly territory, at the same time searching for a suitable place to force-land. As altitude ran out I selected a reasonably soft-looking Tunisian ploughed field, switched off the fuel, flipped down the flaps and bellied in. As the dust settled, I saw 72 circling overhead and fondly hoped they had my position pinpointed.

As I climbed out of the cockpit pondering my next move, I heard a bullet ricochet off the engine cowl. I stood not on the order of my going but took off at once towards a small dry stone wall which seemingly offered the only shelter. Covering some fifty yards in record time, my flying boots skimmed the wall in true Olympic hurdling style. I cowered down behind the stones wondering what next to do when a voice said, 'Cum over 'ere, mate.'

I couldn't see anyone around and asked where.

A British tin hat emerged fleetingly out of the ground a short distance away. 'Ere,' said its owner.

He moved aside as I scrambled on hands and knees to a tiny slit trench and fell in. My feet trod on something soft and I found myself standing on a second occupant. He was fast asleep with one hand dutifully clutching his rifle. He never even stirred as we trampled on him.

''E's bin on all night,' remarked my rescuing Tommy, who went on to explain that his observation trench was a forward outpost of the Empire with nothing British between ourselves and the Wehrmacht except my grounded Spit.

Tommy cranked up a field blower announcing that he'd 'got the pilot 'ere, sir'.

The telephone told us to report to Battalion Headquarters which after scrambling through the rocks, we found in a small railway station.[1] An imperturbable lieutenant-colonel bade me good morning, handing me the army's solution to all imponderables, a steaming mug of tea. We discussed the next move which I suggested should be if possible the salvage of my parachute and flying helmet which at the time were irreplaceable in Africa. Accordingly, the Colonel organised a party of half a dozen armed Tommies and we wriggled over no man's land to the Spit. I dragged out all the retrievable gear from the cockpit and pushed the IFF destruct button.[2]

---

[1] Regrettably, I do not recall which infantry regiment this battalion belonged to.
[2] (IFF) Interpretation Friend or FOR radar responder with classified frequency exchange. Codeword, Canary.

Somehow we got back without any undue German interruption.

The Colonel generously provided his large Humber staff car with a driver and an escort of three Tommies for my transport back to base. As we entered the valley from Medjez to Souk I saw twelve fighters at low level heading directly towards us. My aircraft recognition being considerably more on the ball than my army comrades I yelled:

'Stop! Messerschmitts.'

The driver screeched to a halt and we dived into a ditch as the leading Me 109 opened fire. With some relief we saw it was a one pass deal as our assailants maintained their easterly course. Two shells had hit the front of the car but it had not sustained any major damage so we continued on our way. Ahead of us at Souk el Arba several columns of dense black smoke curled skywards. We neared the airfield and our worst fears were confirmed. The 109's had bombed and strafed the dispersals, catching a number of our Spitfires refuelling after the first mission.

Abortive attempts were made to douse the flames, but with no fire tenders the stricken aircraft had to burn themselves out. Expecting a repeat attack we sorted out some serviceable Spitfires and posted a standing patrol over the airfield. In mid-afternoon we heard the sound of diving radial engines and out of the clouds peeled a *Staffel* of Fw 190's. The flight of 152 patrolling above tried to intercept but were outpaced and one of their Spits was shot down. The 190's came down, strafing everything in sight. In the short time we'd been at Souk, we hadn't had time to dig any slit trenches so we just hit the deck. David Cox and I nudged together for mutual protection as we saw a 190 open up on us. We heard the shells slicing the ground as they whizzed past uncomfortably close. A few yards away a stack of petrol in a shallow ditch seared up in a sheet of flames, roasting alive two airmen who had misguidedly sought refuge nearby.

The day's activities had cost 72 seven aircraft destroyed, and the other squadrons about the same. Ronnie Lees called the squadron commanders together for his nightly pow-pow declaring in his forthright Australian way that, 'It seems the Hun wants us out of here, but we've news for him, we're staying!' When Ronnie dug his heels in they stayed dug; we knew that, if the Hun didn't.

With nightfall I sank exhausted on my bed. The calendar showed it was my sister Joy's 21st birthday. I imagined that whatever party she may have had that day, it couldn't possibly resemble mine.

We impatiently awaited replacement aircraft for our wrecked Spitfires and the Squadrons had to combine resources to mount credible fighting units. Even so, we could rarely put up formations of more than nine or ten aircraft. The remaining week of November saw hectic action on every mission. Most of it took place in the Beja, Mateur, Tebourba salient where 1st Army was locked in conflict with Von Arnim's panzers.

Our chariot of the time was the tropicalized Spitfire Mk VB equipped with a Vokes engine air intake dust filter which knocked off a bit of speed, but as most of the action was below 20,000-feet the aircraft performed very creditably. After several days our replacement Spitfires arrived and 72's score began to mount as the boys got stuck in. Inside the first ten days or so no less than nine of the squadron's pilots weighed in with at least one confirmed kill each, most of the victims being Me 109's and Ju 88's. For the first time we encountered the Italian Air Force when a raid of Savoia 79's escorted by Macchi 202's tried to bomb army targets at Tebourba. We broke up the formations and wound up in a series of individual scraps, but on the day it was difficult to assess the claims owing to extensive cloud in the area.

The advance units of 1st Army were less than thirty miles from Tunis but their supply lines were stretched to the limit. At the same time the Germans were daily pouring in reinforcements from Sicily to stem the advance. To maintain the British momentum everything depended on rapid support by the residue of 1st Army's troops which had not yet landed in North Africa. With Bône now secured it was expected by the Army and RAF that these urgently awaited convoys would be landed at this port to maintain the impetus.

Unfortunately the Royal Navy declined to expose their ships to the threat of air attack beyond 4° East. This attitude no doubt stemmed from the considerable losses in ships suffered in the previous two years during the attempts to relieve the besieged island of Malta, but on those occasions there was no air cover. The situation in November 1942 was very different since the Navy could have called on at least a dozen land-based RAF fighter squadrons to provide continuous air protection between Algiers and Bône. At this crucial time therefore the great weight of 1st Army's back-up was disembarked at Algiers and had to proceed over three hundred time-consuming miles through mountainous country before joining up with the front line troops. Such also was the fate which befell the desperately needed ground crews of the RAF fighter squadrons.

The lamentable naval decision not to unload troops at Bône delayed for a couple of precious weeks the Army's ability to consolidate its forces for the advance on Tunis. By the time the back-up arrived, together with our own ground crews, the winter had started.

Torrential rain pelted down day and night. The dusty Tunisian countryside became a morass of mud. Everything was bogged down and all hopes of 1st Army taking Tunis were shelved. Movement of anything at Souk el Arba was difficult and operation of the aircraft particularly so. Take-offs and landings had to be executed with elevator hard back as the mud sucked at the wheels tending to pull the nose down. All taxiing required the weight of two airmen on the tail plane to prevent the propeller chewing the ground. One unfortunate airman of 152 Squadron on this duty was not fleet enough to get clear before the aircraft took off. Becoming airborne the alarmed pilot felt weird control movements and in seeking the reason happened to glance in his rear mirror to be confronted with the view of an air force blue backside appended to his tailplane. Panicking somewhat, he made a rapid half circuit followed by a rather rough landing. The gallant airman, who had hung on tenaciously throughout the short flight, was finally unshipped as the Spit hit the deck. He was lucky enough to get away with just a broken arm, but not surprisingly his nerve went for a Burton and he was deservedly cas-evac'd back to Blighty.

Christmas 1942 arrived. All day long the rain pelted down and no flying was possible. Squelching through the mud we prepared to make the best of it. David Cox had bartered an enormous turkey from a local Arab with which to celebrate the great day. Since it was still alive he kept it tied to his camp bed until the day of execution, but when eventually cooked for our feast we felt this splendid bird need not have been sacrificed. We couldn't get our teeth into the meat which must have seen twenty summers. A bounty arrived from the Ordnance Corps of one bottle of gin per head. In the absence of any suitable alternative, the potency of this overseas proof liquor was diluted with tangerine juice. To ensure continuity of the festive celebration, Derek Forde persuaded the Foreign Legion to part with a quantity of so-called *vin ordinaire* which, there being no other containers available, had to be transported in petrol tins. A mouthful of this pernicious gut rot, flavoured with the fumes of 100 octane gasoline, was sufficient to recede the hairline untold inches. We huddled in our dripping tents, knocking back the witch's brew, and toasted the health of faraway kin.

Next day the rain stopped. We strapped on our mud-smeared Spits and staggered aloft to resume the war. Through bloodshot optics we sought to vent our hate on any hapless foe sufficiently misguided to disturb our brittle equilibrium.

CHAPTER ELEVEN

'A STRIP OF WIRE NETTIN'

'My Spit was so full of holes I figured I was flyin' a strip of wire nettin'!'

Pilot Officer H S 'Lou' Lewis, RAF later USAAF

One of the second tour pilots who joined 72 after we left Biggin Hill was Warrant Officer H W 'Chas' Charnock DFM. Chas was a remarkable character whose RAF career had been chequered to say the least. A product of Harrow and Cranwell, he had been court martialled and dismissed from the service for a low flying offence in the early thirties. On the outbreak of war he was accepted back in the air force as a sergeant pilot and proceeded to win a Distinguished Flying Medal in the Battle of Britain.

Thirty-seven years of age when 72 Squadron hit Tunisia in 1942, Chas was not only the oldest squadron pilot in North Africa, but as a natural aviator he ranked with the best. Those wingmen who formated on him swore that when penetrating thousands of feet of cloud he never once looked at his instruments but gazed around everywhere except in the cockpit. He flew by the seat of his pants. He knew instinctively his attitude in climb and dive from the note of the engine, and had a needle and ball turn instrument built into his backside.

Chas went to work straightaway. With his chocolate and silver coloured old Harrovian silk scarf a permanent feature around his neck, he charged into action to the considerable discomfiture of the adjacent *Luftwaffe*. Within a few days he demolished a 109E, three 109F's and a further 109F probably destroyed. In the last action he was caught by an enterprising 109 and had his wing blown off; an unusual occurrence with a Spitfire. He baled out near Tebourba and was returned by the Army next day after a boozy night with the local battalion.

Chas's meteoric antics continued for another two weeks until, on 18th December, we flew area cover for two American bomber formations. Twenty-four Bostons and an equal number of B17 Fortresses escorted by P 38 Lightnings attacked the German-held port at Biserte and the airfield complex at Mateur. Not surprisingly, the *Luftwaffe* reacted in strength to this lethal penetration of their air space and battle was joined in a big way. Initially we had some trouble with the Lightning escort whose pilots of the twin-engined, twin-tailed P 38's were experiencing their first war combats. Their aircraft recognition was suspect and in surmounting this deficiency they just assumed that any single-engined, single-tailed fighter was hostile. Anxious to blood themselves, they homed in on friendly and enemy fighters alike, and we spent some anxious moments dodging their headlong attacks.

Having shaken off our Allies we got stuck into the *Luftwaffe*. Robby Robertson and Chas accounted for a 109F in quick time before a *staffel* of Fw 190's joined the party. One of these Chas unceremoniously blew up before being set upon by four others. Chas's Spit was badly shot up, his engine seized and he fell out of the fight. Nobody saw him descend and as time passed with no news of him, hopes for his safety gradually faded. Some days later to our huge delight, he cheerfully turned up, bandages round his head and his left arm in a sling. He said he pranged down near Djebel Abiod which he knew was in enemy territory to be greeted by a shifty-looking Arab. Producing a golden sovereign[1] and using Arabian semaphore he bribed the son of Allah to conduct him to the British lines.

After a short distance Chas had a sixth sense that he was being led in the wrong direction so he changed his tactics, drew his revolver, and fired a slug between his guide's feet, indicating that the next round would be

[1] All aircrews in North Africa were issued with five gold sovereigns in their evasion kits. Gold was considered to have a higher bribe attraction to the natives than the local paper currency.

more accurate. The Arab got the message and the escape direction rapidly altered some ninety degrees. The amended trek proved more successful since it led directly to a British Army patrol.

Chas's wounds were severe enough to require treatment at base hospital and it was three long months before he returned to 72. His aggressive exploits thoroughly earned a Distinguished Flying Cross which was awarded shortly afterwards. It was ridiculous that a chap of his calibre and training, leading sections and flights daily into action, should not be commissioned. Before he left for Algiers I told him I was recommending him for such.

His reaction was typical; he remarked that since rejoining the air force several commanders had tried this exercise but that his 'heinous crime of low flying' was not forgotten and that the applications 'always bounced back like dud cheques'. I countered that we were now overseas and not in the UK, and that perhaps he stood more chance of success. Eventually, he was interviewed by an Air Officer who in the distant past had been a fellow cadet at Cranwell. The issue was then beyond doubt and Chas emerged from hospital a full blown pilot officer, DFC,DFM.

As the *Luftwaffe* built up its strength in Tunisia, we recognised familiar adversaries among their *Jagdgeschwaders*.[2] JG 53 'Pik As', flew in from Sicily after recent operations against Malta. Readily identifiable by the Ace of Spades insignia on its Me 109F's, the unit's *staffels* had been a thorn in our side over the Channel area since 1940. JG 2, the 'Richthofen' Fw 190 outfit, flew in from Northern France and based on Biserte.

It was some time before we had any assistance from ground control radar. When a mobile set ultimately became operational, its performance, despite the expertise of experienced controllers, was minimal. The effective operating range was limited to about fifty miles, and the target height assessment, compared with the UK performance, was woefully inadequate.

During the first month of the campaign in Northern Tunisia, the concentrated zone of air operations was dictated by the close proximity of the front lines to the *Luftwaffe* airfields and the German supply ports at Biserte, Ferryville and Tunis. Almost every mission to this area resulted in a clash of opposing fighters. In this environment 72 had a ball. In four

[2] Jagdgeschwader (JG); A tighter wing of up to six squadrons.

weeks the squadron accounted for twenty-one enemy aircraft destroyed plus eight probables. The Army confirmed many of our claims over the battlefield, and at this particular time, because of the relatively low altitude plus the clear visibility in which we were operating, successful combats were easy to witness and substantiate by fellow pilots.

The deficit side was inevitable. On one hairy sortie to Mateur the squadron mixed it with some fifteen 109F's and after a scrap in which three pilots registered probable kills we withdrew in scattered sections. Johnny Lowe, a promising young pilot who had scored with a Ju 88 a couple of days before, was missing. No one could account for him, yet he was found some days later with his crashed Spitfire in the hills not far from the field at Souk. He had been shot down but his assailant was never seen. Shortly afterwards, 72 conducted a low level escort of two reconnaissance Hurricanes from 241 Squadron which wound up at 2,000-feet near Biserte. We ran straight into a standing patrol of Me 109F's which took up the challenge as our A flight turned into them. A dog fight erupted and I got a close burst on a 109 as it swung past. There were no flames but dense black smoke poured out of its cowling as it dived from 1,500-feet behind a hill. Before I could see the result another 109 jumped my No 4, Sergeant A Mottram. Three of us turned to drive it off but Mottram didn't return. In the same action Sergeant F M Browne's Spit was seen to crash in flames clobbered, we believed, by a direct hit from enemy flak.

These casualties in the space of a couple of days were depressing but mercifully were the worst we endured in the campaign. All four unfortunate pilots had just started their first tour of operations. Inexperience must in some part have contributed to the loss of at least three of them.

A number of casualties were suffered by the other squadrons as well as 72, but nevertheless a magnificent offensive spirit pervaded 324 Wing. Much of it stemmed from our superb commander Ronnie Lees who in the early days carried the entire logistical task without any administrative help. Apart from coordinating the operational flying requirements he organized the continuing supplies of fuel, ammunition, replacement aircraft and pilots, and a multitudinous selection of vital support commodities ranging across the board through the acquisition of medical facilities, transport and rations. Ronnie never seemed to sleep; he was everywhere urging us to maximum effort and dishing out encouragement to all ranks wherever he went. In spite of all his onerous responsibilities he found time to fly with us whenever he could. He was hugely satisfied on one of these trips to weigh into a Savoia 79 bomber which he destroyed with relish. To add to Ronnie's burdens the key post of wing leader was vacant and he had no immediate senior lieutenant with whom to share the load. Eventually the slot was filled when Wing Commander George 'Sheep' Gilroy DFC and bar, arrived from 325 Wing.

At the turn of the year aerial activity was even more intense. The Navy at long last decided it was now safe enough to bring some of the merchant convoys to Bône. The strengthened Luftwaffe reacted immediately. For two hectic days it flung in relays of Ju 87 Stukas, heavily escorted by Me 109's, in determined attempts to sink the ships at anchor in the harbour. At the same time Bône airfield was bombed and strafed but Piet Hugo and his squadrons of 322 Wing were equal to the task. The Stukas in particular suffered severe casualties after which the attacks were reduced to night bombing by singleton raiders. The nett result of the German effort was one oil tanker set on fire in the harbour and some superficial damage to the airfield.

In 324 Wing we worked flat out with each squadron mounting a minimum of four missions a day. Operations embraced every duty in the fighter envelope; freelance sweeps, standing patrols, reconnaissance escort and bomber cover followed in rapid succession. Most of the ops were in wing strength of two squadrons aggressively led by Sheep Gilroy.

No 72 reefed into the action with devastating impact and my faith in the experience of the second tour pilots paid off with interest. It was also encouraging to see success spread across the board and not just vested in a few individuals. Inside three days, Owen Hardy, Pilot Officer Stone and our American Lou Lewis each belted a Fw 190 to destruction; Alan Gear, Red Hunter and Sergeant Griffiths all clobbered Stukas. Our red-headed Scotsman, Steve Daniel, known to most as 'Danny' and to some as 'Dangerous' Daniel, helped himself to a Me 109 and a Fw 190. Not to be outdone Hardy, Jupp and Smith most unchivalrously ganged up on a 190 which ultimately gave up the ghost and crashed inverted.

Fw 190 – Calais – 'not enough deflection'.

Brian Kingcome and Jamie Rankin, Biggin Hill, summer 1942.

Roy Hussey, Chas Charnock, unknown, on board Fort Maclaughlin.

Mickey Rook, OC 43 Squadron, Tunisia 1943.

Piet Hugo and Razz Berry. Tunisia 1943.

'A bite to eat' at 'Euston'. Early dispersal.

Souk el Arba, after strafing by 109s, November 1940.

72 Squadron at Souk el Arba: (L to R) Forde, Daniel and RWO.

RWO and David Cox, Souk el Arba, Tunisia, January 1943 - mutual congratulations on awards of bars to DFC

'The Sexton' W/0 Alan Gear, 72 Squadron, Souk el Khemis, Tunisia 1943.

'Phantom' Farrish, Engineer Officer 72 Squadron, Souk el Khemis 1943.

Steve Daniel and David Cox.

72 Squadron dispersal. Souk el Khemis, Tunisia 1943.

(L to R) Derek Forde, Jimmy Corbin, 'Reuter' McCaul, 'Chem' Le Cheminant and Pete Fowler.

George Malan

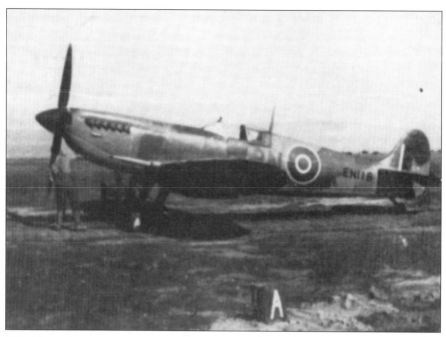

RWO's Spitfire Mark IX, RN-A, 72 Squadron, Souk el Khemis 1943.

'Chem' Le Cheminant, Lou Lewis and Steve Daniel, 72 Squadron, Tunisia.

Pat Lardner-Burke DFC, OC No 1 Squadron.

Squadron Leader Roger Bushell, CO of 92 Squadron until he was shot down and imprisoned in Stalag Luft III. He was in charge of the Escape Committee and organized the 'Great Escape' and subsequently executed by the Gestapo.

Drawing of the author in October 1940 by Orde.

Target area in the raid on Heligoland.

RWO. Post-war photograph 1948.

72 Squadron pilots and Engineer Officer, Souk el Khemis 1943.

Battle of Britain reunion. (Left to right) Jamie Rankin, Paddy Barthropp, Bobby Oxspring, Sailor Malan, the host (at White Hart Brasted) Lt Cdr T Preston RNVR, Brian Kingcome, Tubby Mayne, Tony Bartley and Bob Stanford-Tuck.

To herald the New Year, Sheep Gilroy led the wing of 72 and 111 Squadrons on an escort of 241 Squadron's Hurribombers to attack a Wehrmacht headquarters in the Tunis area. A pack of Me 109's sought to interrupt the proceedings and a sizzling dog fight ensued. We had the bounce on them as Sheep unceremoniously despatched one. David Cox claimed a damaged, and the target at which I fired dived off towards Tunis apparently unscathed. Wheeling back over Pont du Fahs, I saw another 109 beneath me which headed for the deck. In a twisting action at nought feet I fired and my target's propeller stopped. I pulled off as it made a hurried crash landing on the bundu. Post-war records revealed that the 109 pilot was *Feldwebel* Anton Hafner of JG 51, the *Luftwaffe*'s top scoring pilot in Tunisia. He was wounded badly enough to be out of action for six months.

One evening Ronnie Lees told George Nelson-Edwards of 93 Squadron and myself to take our Spits the following day and get the hell out of it on a 48-hour furlough. There being little choice of venues we collected our pay allowance books and homed in on Algiers. Maison Blanche as usual was a Piccadilly Circus of planes, and on landing George and I scorned the use of the visiting aircraft park and headed for 43 Squadron's dispersal. We taxied in and parked among the Hurricanes. As I killed the engine and took off my mask and helmet I spied the imposing figure of Mickey Rook, 43's boss, striding towards me intent on delivering a rocket for illicit parking. I grinned at him and when he recognised me all was forgiven.

'What ho, what ho, the dreaded Ox,' he greeted. 'Be our guest.' Mickey led the way to 43's dispersal. George and I were most impressed. It was a solid building and actually had a roof on it, which after our tented existence on the plains of Tunisia was luxury indeed. Mickey apologized for his impending absence for the next two hours since he was due to fly a convoy patrol. He handed us over to the generous hospitality of his officers headed by the senior flight commander Freddie Lister. It appeared that our arrival had coincided with that of a large consignment of champagne. Since Mickey was a member of a well known family of wine merchants in Nottingham it wasn't difficult to imagine how this cargo of liquid gold had been wangled. Apparently the connections and influence stretched at least as far as Algiers.

While Mickey bored his tedious holes in the Mediterranean sky Freddie Lister uncorked some bottles. Never had bubbly been consumed in such a worthy cause or tasted so good. By the time Mickey returned, his off duty pilots and guests were in cracking form; so much so it was unanimously agreed that it was unthinkable that the rest of the evening should be wasted on base. The enterprising members of 43 provided luxurious and much needed hot showers and for the first time in two months I climbed into my best uniform.

Mickey led a couple of carloads down town. Bracketing the target we homed in on the Kasbah, legendary refuge of film star Charles Boyer. This notorious citadel of stateless persons was forbidding in its lightless, narrow streets and the conspicuous absence of anyone around. We had the feeling that many eyes were watching us and were glad we weren't on foot. Deciding that the district offered no signs of scintillating entertainment, we retreated back to civilization. Following some hilarious double tracking up and down the darkened Algiers streets we found, after numerous queries in fractured French, a gaily lit United States services club. Unfortunately the bar stocked only gassy American beer and even that was rationed to two tins per throat. A couple of friendly American air force officers opined that the best joint in town was a dive known as the Sphinx, so without further ado we set out to track it down.

On arrival a tough-looking doorman relieved us of some money; he didn't seem to care what sort of lucre it was as long as it crinkled. Inside the place was packed as every uniform of the western alliance ebbed and flowed in all directions. The tide rose highest at the bar where a scrum five deep demanded service in a variety of languages over the strains of accordian music wafting from an indeterminate source. A large peroxided female, most of her squeezed into a dress more appropriate to a ballerina in *Swan Lake*, assured us in French that we had the great fortune to enter the finest *maison de passe* west of the Pyramids. This called for a drink, so we formed a wedge and shoved for the bar. After fifteen minutes or so of concentrated scrimmaging we emerged triumphant with a large pernod apiece. Flitting among the throng were bevies of garishly clad harpies, whose strenuous endeavours over the preceding two months since the Allied invasion were reflected in their dead pan features.

We peered at the seething multitude through a fog of tobacco smoke and decided we were on a bum steer. We were too exhausted to take on another loose maul for a drink, so breathing aniseed fumes at each other we plumped for the more congenial atmosphere of 43 Squadron's bar back at base.

Since I'd been the only one on 72 to get a break from Souk el Arba, I felt I owed my chaps a spot of compensation. Next day Mickey lent me some transport and I steamed off for the most highly recommended liquor store in Algiers. When I entered the premises the only other customer was an American Air Force Brigadier-General who had his back to me. He had a shipping order of bottles already stacked on the counter and as they were being packed he turned round to me, stuck out his hand and announced;

'The name's Doolittle, how's your handle?'

As our arms pumped I confirmed from his many medal ribbons that he was indeed the James Doolittle of Tokyo fame the previous year. He now commanded the North West African Strategic Air Force which included the B17 Bombardment Groups.

He chatted to me as I purchased as much decent brandy as my meagre allowances would permit. We discussed the recent war events and I mentioned that we had recently flown cover for his Fortresses in Tunisia. He told me quite candidly that he was not satisfied with the accuracy of the bombing so far, and that he himself would lead the next operation. True to his word, a couple of weeks later he led his Forts in a raid on Ferryville and 72 again provided cover. The bombing was deadly and clobbered an ammunition ship in the harbour. The explosion lifted the ship clear of the water where it split in two, the bow coming down on the jetty and the stern splashing into the sea.

During my short absence from the squadron, 72 had not been idle. Several pilots had notched up more kills on the scoreboard. In one breezy action Lou Lewis got separated from his flight and was set upon by four Macchi 202's who scissored him in pairs from each side. Lou could not break from one pair without being attacked from behind by the other. He tried to shake them off by flying flat out at ground level but to no avail. His Spitfire was holed so many times that he 'figured he was flyin' a strip of wire nettin'. Finally, in desperation, and with gear retracted, he rammed down straight ahead on the deck at a speed approaching 200-mph. On impact his aircraft disintegrated but miraculously he survived, albeit sustaining a rather nasty head injury.

Lou's prang was a classic example of an adage as old as flying itself: 'Any landing you walk away from is a good one!'

CHAPTER TWELVE

'A FIGHTER PILOT'S BREAKFAST'

'A fighter pilot's breakfast – two cigarettes and a puke'

Major Steve Turner, USAAF, later USAF

Being unable to occupy Tunis before the German strength had built up was a bitter disappointment to the Allies. The Allied Command grossly underestimated the Wehrmacht's ability to speedily reinforce the area by air and at night from readily accessible bases in Sicily. Some units of 1st Army advanced tantalizingly close to their objective, but lacking support of substantial armour and heavy artillery the infantry could not contain the superior enemy counter-actions. Valentine tanks of the 17/21st Lancers in concert with the Honeys and Shermans of the American 13th Armoured Regiment were no match for the Panzer III's and IV's and were soundly repulsed in critical clashes. Retreat from the Tunis plain to more defensible emplacements to the west was inevitable.

It is sobering to reflect that within twenty-four hours, in a gallant attempt to capture the small town of Djedeida only fourteen miles from Tunis, the 2nd Battalion the Hampshire Regiment suffered over 580 casualties from a strength of 800; more than twice the roll of the entire Falklands campaign in 1982. From other advanced positions, the West Kents near Jefna, and the 2nd Paras at Oudna, had likewise to retreat with fatalities approaching those of the Hampshires.

The misery of the retrenching troops was intensified by repeated dive bombing attacks from Stukas and fighter bombers. As usual when the Army was subjected to such treatment the mournful cry went up, 'Where wuz the Air Force?' We could tell them. We were constantly over the battlefield engaged in the most frenzied turkey shoot the war had yet spewed up.

Even if our unreliable radar could pick up the enemy formations so engaged, the *Luftwaffe's* strike aircraft in some cases were based less than twenty miles from the harassed battalions and could take oil', strike and land in less than half an hour. This left insufficient time for our fighters to scramble from base to counter the threat. Nevertheless, our offensive patrols over the battlefield registered a high proportion of interceptions on enemy strikes, and much chagrin to the vulnerable infantry was effectively forestalled.

Fresh Allied units constantly flowed to the front from the rear areas, some American forces travelling over 1,000-miles from their disembarkation ports at Oran and Casablanca, but the onset of winter bogged down any concerted offensive on Tunis.

The cloying mud surface of the airfield at Souk el Arba was seriously hampering operations and Ronnie Lees cast around for an alternative. His search ended at Souk el Khemis where the sandy, fast draining surface had the added advantage of being some fifteen miles nearer the front lines. The area was big enough to contain the construction of four airfields with Sommerfeld wire tracked runways. Named after London railway stations the strips were known as Euston, Paddington, Marylebone and King's Cross. The capacity of the complex ensured a sizeable reinforcement of fighter wings from the rear areas and more squadrons began to move in. 72 commandeered the small Khemis railway station as squadron headquarters and set up shop to operate from Euston.

Luftwaffe fighters were beginning to range at higher altitudes and it was increasingly difficult to get at them with our tropicalized Spit Vs. The answer was the Spitfire IX and Razz Berry took 81 Squadron from Bône to fetch a shipment which had just arrived at Gibraltar. Our envy didn't last long before Ronnie Lees informed us that 72 were to proceed hot foot for the next batch.

Leaving the squadron in the capable hands of the adjutant, Tiny le Petit, the pilots set off by road to Constantine and thence by USAAF Dakota to Gib. We spent a few days testing our new chariots and enjoying the luxuries of civilization. We also took the opportunity to re-equip with much needed new flying gear, including priceless parachutes.

Riding back to Euston it was sheer joy to feel the surging power of the Spitfire Mark IX over the Mark V. We hadn't realised how much we'd missed it since Biggin Hill days six months before. We were greeted by our engineer officer 'Phantom' Farrish who got highly steamed up to see that our brand new steeds were untropicalized in that no Vokes air intake filters were fitted. Farrish was the ideal plumber for an overseas campaign. He had no time for paper work and was usually to be found, sleeves rolled up, ministering his mechanical talent to the most errant Merlin of the day. Within twenty-four hours he had designed and made a mesh filter which could be hung over the air intake for all ground operations. The improvisation proved most efficient and an adequate number were constructed in the field workshop to equip the whole squadron.

Since 'Farrish's Phantom Filters', as they were immediately dubbed, could not be carried on missions because of the air restriction to the engines at altitude, they had to have some means of ejection after take-off. A Bowden cable, hitherto designed for the release of night flares from a fuselage tube, was misappropriated for the purpose. Procedures were evolved whereby after the squadron was airborne the flights would fly low over the up wind end of the runway and on an order from the leader the pilots jettisoned the filters. These were collected by the ground crews who, on the return of the squadron, hooked them back in place before the aircraft taxied in. Farrish's filters proved so successful that they were subsequently manufactured in large numbers at base workshops in Algiers.

The second stage supercharger on the Merlin 61 had an automatic barometric control gauged to cut in at 19,000-feet. Since barometric instruments are notoriously imprecise, the effect on a squadron climbing for altitude at high power settings meant that twelve superchargers cut in at slightly different times. The effect on the formation with these widely fluctuating power settings was like shuffling a pack of cards and trying to keep the same suit together. To overcome this discrepancy, we decided to climb well above the automatic setting utilising the manual override. On a radio order from the leader we flipped the 'auto' switch and cut the superchargers in together. We were then able to contend with the foe at high altitudes, but it was prudent to keep the knowledge of our capability from him as long as possible. Bearing in mind the efficiency of the enemy's 'Y' service,[1] we devised a code for 2nd supercharger engagement. The formation leader's instruction for simultaneous action by the other pilots was 'Up your pipe'; 'Up your' being the warning, and 'Pipe' being the executive command to cut in. The stratagem had the desired effect and 'Pipe' sent the squadron soaring aloft like a pack of homesick angels.

Early in the New Year, Ian Krohn and Derek Forde became tour-expired and were posted. Their replacements were promoted from within the squadron, David Cox taking over one flight and Dangerous Daniel the other. Both had served on the squadron since Biggin Hill days and since arrival in Tunisia had considerably enhanced their records.

In his early days big Danny didn't exactly fly a Spitfire, he poled it in to the positions he wanted by copious use of all controls. His landings were a series of hairy incidents. On more than one occasion he forgot to turn on his gun button to safe, which omission initiated the triggers as he heaved the stick back against his massive chest. This final gesture before touch down on squared tyres, spewed forth a hail of cannon fire which galvanized airfield strollers into frantic search of cover. Nevertheless, Danny proved a more lethal protagonist to the *Luftwaffe* than the RAF as he proceeded to wreak mayhem through opposing forces. He was destined to take over 72 from me, and finished the war with a total of sixteen enemy aircraft destroyed.

David Cox, a Battle of Britain veteran from 19 Squadron in Douglas Bader's wing at Duxford, was a natural leader. Quick and aggressive he lost no time in blasting down half a dozen German aircraft to augment his record of the previous two years. Later in the war he resumed alliance with me, leading No 1 Squadron in my wing at Manston.

[1] 'Y' Service: Intelligence derived from inteception of enemy radio broadcasts' a 'Listening' service.

I was fortunate to have Coxy and Danny as flight commanders in 72. They were largely responsible for the squadron's dynamic record in the Tunisian campaign.

In the meantime, continuing the bright start he'd made at Biggin Hill, Robbie Robertson weighed in to the action with more successful kills and brought his personal score to six enemy fighters destroyed. Unfortunately, in a hectic dogfight over Beja, a cannon shell slashed into his cockpit blasting a splinter of debris through one of his eyes. Half blinded, he made a courageous crash-landing, and it was some consolation shortly afterwards when his hard-earned DFC came through. We bade a sad farewell to Robbie; he'd done a great job.

In the intensity of the North African operations, our first tour pilots took their example from the hard bitten old sweats and learnt their trade fast. As they progressed into deadly combatants, their individual successes blossomed. None more so than Sergeant Roy Hussey, who had a sensitive nose for trouble and a natural instinct to do the right thing. Roy shot down six enemy aircraft in the Tunisian campaign and was deservedly awarded a DFM. Shortly afterwards he was commissioned and still serving with 72 went on to increase his score in Italy to $13^1/_2$ destroyed. He was promoted to flight commander and earned a DFC. It was tragic that he was killed in a landing accident to his Mustang with 19 Squadron in 1945.

When all personnel of 72 had finally assembled in Tunisia, the establishment was deficient only in one post, that of the squadron intelligence officer. Consequently the important time consuming duties of the briefing and debriefing requirements, compiling operational records and composing combat reports had to be undertaken in turn by various pilots who could find time to spare between their operational sorties. The squadron's returns in this sphere therefore tended to be inaccurate and sketchy.

On a visit one day to the squadron orderly room I witnessed one of the very young airman clerks listening to a full ten-minute radio broadcast of the BBC overseas news. As the bulletin concluded the airman turned round to a loaded typewriter and without a single error hammered out news sheets for distribution to various elements of the unit. Much impressed by such a display of memory and initiative I promptly enlisted this aircraftman's talents to perform the duties of intelligence officer.

The airman's name was Michael McCaul. Since the job required mobility he was provided with the only form of transport available, a 250cc Matchless motor-cycle. Not having driven this type of conveyance before, Mike nevertheless hurled himself into the task with boundless enthusiasm. His initial forays from headquarters to the flight dispersals were interlaced with a series of prangs as he parted company with his errant steed, but his determination to fulfil his newly acquired duties overcame all obstacles. As the aircraft parked after missions Mike moved along the flight line interrogating the pilots in turn, and his phenomenal memory resulted in precise operational records and combat reports being produced with minimum delay. His impact on the squadron intelligence processes was startling and his eagerness to obtain the gen for onwards transmission earned him the nickname of 'Reuter' McCaul.

In a very short time Mike mastered not only the demands of squadron intelligence but also the art of controlling a motor bike. He soon became an indispensable member of the squadron. Despite raised eyebrows that I'd had the temerity to employ an airman on duties which, because of security aspects were decreed for officers only, I recommended that Mike be interviewed for commissioning at a higher echelon. He successfully passed a selection board at Middle East Air Force and emerged as a fully fledged pilot officer in the RAF intelligence branch. Later on he was posted to Iraq, where he embarked on a long career in security intelligence work.

In 1975 he was made a Companion of the Order of Saint Michael and Saint George, a much deserved honour.

No 72 Squadron was a superb team. Combat drills were second nature and we had no fears of being bounced. All fighter pilots have good eyesight, but those of Owen Hardy and George Malan, younger brother of the renowned Sailor, were exceptional. Normally flying as section leaders in the flanking flights, they spotted hostile aircraft like long range radars. Such early sightings gave 72 the edge over the opposition, and with the superior climb of our Spit IX's we gained the tactical advantage to initiate attacks. To cite a classic example, on a mission covering Fortresses bombing Biserte, we spotted over twenty Me 109's gaining height to intercept. The early sighting gave us the chance to outclimb the Messerschmitts, and from 34,000-feet we bounced them as they were about to attack. Hussey and Jupp clobbered one apiece, and the Forts were unmolested.

By mid-February the 8th Army had driven the Afrika Korps from the Western Desert into southern Tunisia. Rommel consolidated a 'natural defensive position between the hills and the sea at Mareth. This cued Montgomery into one of his increasingly famous stop and fart situations.

Whilst Monty marked time, the Afrika Korps took advantage of the lull. In a savage assault to protect his supply corridor to Mareth, Rommel launched two Panzer divisions against the US Army on the central front. After a headlong retreat of sixty miles through the Kasserine Pass the Americans, with British help from 1st Army, finally arrested the thrust. For nearly a week the crisis teetered in the balance until, on the brink of success, Rommel unexpectedly withdrew.

Although the Panzer pressure relaxed, the *Luftwaffe* certainly did not. Constant dive-bombing and strafing attacks were directed against precariously-held Allied positions all along the front. In the north, the Guards Brigade had long established an ongoing dispute with the Wehrmacht over a couple of hills near Medjez. Possession of these was considered vital for the domination of the two roads from Medjez to Tunis. The northern knap of the two named Longstop Hill changed hands several times during the campaign and became a prerogative of 2nd Battalion Coldstream Guards. Having battled and gained Longstop on one occasion, the Coldstreamers were relieved by an American battalion who promptly lost possession overnight. Undaunted the Guards turned round and retook the crest; rumour had it that on the next handover the exasperated Coldstreamer CO demanded a receipt. Capture of the other hill to the east of Medjez became the responsibility of 3rd Battalion Grenadier Guards. Their continuing struggle to retain possession inspired such abiding emotion that they bequeathed their name to its title.

Our soldiers' obsession for lofty emplacements was matched only by the determination of the Wehrmacht to deny them the privilege. In search of action our fighter squadrons had only to seek our certain knobbly locations to find our infantry struggling doggedly to acquire or defend a hill. More often than not we found the *Luftwaffe* in attendance, attracted like moths to a candle. Apart from the Guards at Grenadier and Longstop, there were Bald and Green Hills which caused much aggravation for the West Kents, the Buffs and the Argyll and Sutherland Highlanders.

Later in the campaign there was considerable confrontation when Von Arnim struck towards Tebarka in the north. Djebel Abiod, and a neighbouring prominence labelled the Leicester Pimple after its defenders, caused considerable anguish to the Para Brigade, the Sherwood Foresters, the Lincolns and the Durham Light Infantry. Escorting a squadron of Hurribombers to clobber nearby Jefna railway station during this blitz, 72 suffered a nasty setback when Pilot Officer Jupp and Sergeant Smith collided and crashed near the target, both being killed. We never fathomed the reason for the accident, but collision between close-flying aircraft was an ever present hazard for fighter squadrons. Less than forty-eight hours later the wing leader, Sheep Gilroy, and Edward Mortimer-Rose, rammed into each other over Khemis. Morty spun in and died, but Sheep was more fortunate and managed to bale out with only slight injuries. Even this didn't end the spate. On a reconnaissance escort to the Beja area, 152 Squadron's Flight Lieutenant Smith and Pilot Officer Gilroy collided, the latter tragically being killed, but Smithy managed to crash-land.

With the establishment of the Mareth line all Allied and Axis combatant forces were concentrated in Tunisia. The air war hotted up as German and Italian squadrons, hitherto supporting Rommel's Afrika Korps, boosted their counterparts already in the area. At the same time the Desert Air Force came in range of the extended battle zone and threw in its considerable weight. The sky became quite congested as swarms of fighter squadrons, Allied and Axis alike, ranged the length of the country. Heavily escorted Allied bomber formations struck at every conceivable target as the offensive reached a climax. Although enemy air activity also noticeably increased, Allied fighter supremacy reduced the ration of targets available. From Khemis the squadrons ranged further afield, and sweeps as far as Kairouan and Sousse became common.

The Spit IX's of 72 and 81 were in much demand to provide high cover for the non-stop bomber operations. Shortly after the Kasserine debacle, 72 were ordered to Thelepte to provide withdrawal cover for an American A20 bombing mission to Tebaga scheduled for the following day. The order posed some logistical problems since Thelepte had been one of the airfields the Americans had evacuated during the Kasserine rumpus, and had just reoccupied with a fighter group equipped with Spitfire Vs. We had no idea of the American capability to service our aircraft so we resolved to take no chances. Phantom Farrish organized a party of ground crews and, with Reuter McCaul navigating, set out overnight for Thelepte in a convoy of trucks loaded with spares, belts of ammunition and starter batteries. After a traumatic journey packed with incident on the 250-miles of war-scarred roads, they turned up in time to greet our arrival next morning.

In the event the bombing mission was cancelled, and we utilized the day with sweeps to the active Maknassy area. The visibility was lousy, being shrouded in a thick haze, but climbing above it on the first sortie we found a pack of some fifteen Me 109's and Fw 190's about to bounce some American Spitfires. At 23,000-feet this was made to order for our Spit IX's and we waded in to a dogfight where Danny and Owen Hardy clobbered a 109 each with David Cox damaging another. Pete Fowler's aircraft was damaged in the fight but we all got back. A one day stand such as this, over 200-miles from home base, proved too time consuming and we didn't try it again.

Subject as they were to round the clock bombing of their bases, the *Luftwaffe* squadrons were far from intimidated and in fact retaliated in kind. Returning one day from a reconnaissance cover mission we found 152 Squadron on airfield defence battling it out with some Me 109G's bent on a bombing attack at Souk el Arba. Having the height and speed 72 mixed in scattering the formations into individual dogfights. One 109 climbed away east out of the mêlée and I followed it with my wingman, Red Hunter. As it gained height at full bore we were just about at maximum firing range, but not noticeably catching up; Red fired a long burst without effect and ran out of ammunition. We hung on until around 19,000-feet the supercharger cut in sending me close underneath the 109's tail. I let fly and white glycol streamed from the engine as the canopy peeled away and the pilot baled out. He dropped to my left and I saw his parachute blossom. A second later he fell out of the harness and careered earthward leaving a flapping canopy behind. 'Poor bastard,' I thought, and could no longer watch his fateful fall in which he had about three minutes to contemplate the errors of not strapping his chute on tight. He hit the deck behind our lines near Beja, and on recovering his body the Army said his rank was *Oberfeldwebel* (Warrant Officer). I didn't want to know his name.

While the armies were sorting themselves out the air war continued unabated and support for 1st Army was still our primary prerequisite. Covering a squadron of Hurricanes bombing close support targets, 72 intercepted some Me 109's which tried to interfere. We had the jump on them as Danny took his flight down on a formation of four. He and George Malan moved in to clobber a couple which crashed nearby. As the rest of the squadron gave cover another half a dozen 109's appeared beneath and I led the formation down in a copybook bounce. It was a dream set up as we closed range and blasted our targets. Mine shed some bits and hit the deck east of Medjez as Alan Gear worked over another which spun away. The sudden impact split up the rest of the enemy, and in the ensuing mill the squadron damaged three more. Sergeant Sollitt caught a packet in the action, but managed to crash land unhurt behind our lines.

Although 72 mostly dished out punishment, occasions arose when we had to take it. One offensive sweep east of Medjez saw the squadron encounter a mixed gaggle of bomb carrying Ju 88's and Me 110's escorted by Me 109's and Fw 190's bent on attacking Army dispositions in the area. The enemy dived on their targets through a hail of British flak as 72 engaged. Pryth Prytherch belted a 110 while George Malan and Tom Hughes chased another. Drawing close to his target George was severely hit by our own ground fire and though badly wounded managed to pull off a rough crash landing. Nearby Tommies whisked him off to a local field hospital, where the Army surgeons were shocked at the bitterness with which George died cursing all 'pongos'.[2]

One April morning I partook in the fighter pilots' time-honoured custom of two cigarettes for breakfast. Shortly afterwards with my Spit strapped on for the first mission, I cranked up the engine and had immediately to evacuate the cockpit to heave a puke on the bundu. As my stomach vomited for relief, it seemed that the protein diet of hot greased bully I was unwise enough to add to the fags, had been more nauseous than usual. Unfortunately our squadron doctor, Paddy Griffin, witnessed the incongruous exhibition and being Irish couldn't keep his mouth shut. He

[2] Pongos: air force slang for army personnel

carted me off to bed and left me to survive a day of retching enteritis. To add to my misery Ronnie Lees told me I was tour-expired. I didn't want to leave 72 on the Tunisian final lap, but time had caught up.

Before my departure I raked together some statistics. In the five months since arrival in Africa, 72 was the top scoring fighter squadron of the campaign with a tally of fifty-three enemy aircraft destroyed, twenty probables and fifty damaged. A further half dozen victories were added before moving to Malta. Supplementing the air successes was a spate of enemy aircraft and transport annihilated on the ground.

Conversely, our casualties, distressing though they were, had been minimal. Three were killed in action, three were posted as missing, four were wounded and two were killed in a mid air collision.

I had special words of gratitude for the ground crews, whose dedicated efforts ensured a very high standard of aircraft serviceability. Maintenance was achieved in the open, despite extremes of weather ranging from torrential rain to dust storms. From time to time their labours were seriously hampered by dive bombing and strafing attacks from the *Luftwaffe*, but with well chosen expletives they always bounced back smiling.

No 72 Squadron richly earned a number of decorations in the campaign which comprised two bars to the DFC, ten DFC's, one DFM and a BEM (British Empire Medal). The pilots vindicated my confidence in them, and I felt I was entitled to reflect that the squadron had won the Tunisian match by an innings.

CHAPTER THIRTEEN

'POSTED TO HEADQUARTERS'

'So you're posted to headquarters, Bobby – Gad, sir, you must be shit hot!'

Air Marshal Sir Richard Atcherley, KBE, CB, AFC

My next assignment was to HQ 242 Group commanded by Air Commodore K B B 'Bing' Cross, courageous survivor of the *Glorious* sinking in 1940. The Group had the overall responsibility for the direction of RAF and US fighters and fighter bombers in direct support of 1st Army. Ronnie Lees took up the appointment of Senior Air Force Staff Officer of the Group at the same time. His was a clear cut slot, but for myself I hadn't a clue what I was supposed to be doing.

The headquarters consisted of a couple of caravans and a battery of tents situated on one of the Army's cherished hills near Medjez. The whole was connected by miles of field telephone wires none of which, despite frantic cranking, ever seemed to have an answering voice at the other end. In an attempt to ease the situation, some of the connections to the army were routed through some clapped-out French telephone exchanges, and my sole success with these infuriating instruments was an attempt to contact the Grenadier Guards to lay on some air support. Just as I was about to give my wrist a rest from the crank, behold a response:

'Oui?'

'Beja soixante-douze, s'il vous plait.'

'Oui.'

'Est-ce que c'est Beja soixante-douze?'

'Oui.'

Self, aside to friend: 'Oh God, no one speaks the King's English.'

Telephone: 'What the hell do you want, old boy?'

The Allied armies were finally poised for the big push. 'Blood and Guts' Patton took his II Corps to the northern coastal belt with the objective of taking Biserte. The Free French Army were to strike north-east from Pont du Fahs to the Cap Bon peninsula, but the main thrust was that of 1st Army, heavily reinforced by 8th Army artillery and armour, from the Medjez salient to Tunis.

At the Army's favourite ungodly hour of 3am, all hell broke loose. Over 600 guns packed wheel to wheel let fly with a barrage at the opposing Panzer divisions. For a couple of hours 1st Army's artillery pounded the enemy before tanks and infantry surged forward in a dominant charge.

Over the battlefield the sky clouded with Allied tactical bombers and fighters intent on clobbering any hostile forces who deigned to move. The temptation to see what was going on was too much, and Ronnie Lees told me to grab a couple of Spitfires for us to have a dekko. A cloud of dust shrouded the combat area as every wheel the Army possessed churned eastward in pursuit of the disintegrating Wehrmacht.

Suddenly I glimpsed a flight of four fighters beneath us which looked suspiciously like Me 109's. Calling the sighting to Ronnie, I peeled down into a starboard quarter attack. Ronnie followed, and I was just getting nicely into range on the number 4 of the formation when it banked and I saw the United States star on the top side of the port wing. At the time the Americans had a dumb scheme of only carrying their national markings on the port wing, and in this case at least two guys were within a hair's breadth of death because of it. They were in fact green camouflaged P40 Warhawks with silhouettes closely akin to 109's, and I called to Ronnie, 'Break off, they're Yanks'.

I reefed round the break, looked round for Ronnie and spotted him above me. The gallant Group Captain was upside down and rolling out of a loop as I came up on his wing. After we landed he queried, 'What the hell happened, Bobby? We had a beautiful bounce on those Huns.'

My warning call had been garbled, but it conveyed an urgency and seeing me break he followed suit. He never knew until I told him how close we had come to punching a dent in Uncle Sam's air power.

Most of the German troops fought the final battle until they ran out of ammunition. They then surrendered in their thousands and the time arose to see what worthwhile booty they had left around which was worth salvaging. The first priority was to track down any abandoned Fieseler Storches, useful German light communications aircraft which could take off and land in incredibly short distances. The C-in-C, North West African Tactical Air Force, Air Marshal Sir Arthur Coningham had a predilection for these machines, and decreed all those captured as his personal spoils of war. Knowing he could land a Storch in fifty yards, the C-in-C occasionally selected a field of that length disregarding the fact that it was bounded by stone walls at each end. Spare parts, especially propellers, were therefore at a premium.

I grabbed a puddle-jumping Auster and spent eight hours flying to all the recent *Luftwaffe* airfields in Tunisia. The search disclosed three Fieseler Storches, two Me 109's and a Fw 190 which all looked as though, with some attention, they would fly again. Some keen RAF Servicing Commandos helped me pitch into the mysteries of German engineering and we ultimately cranked up a Fieseler Storch at La Marsa near Tunis. Not knowing what would happen I faced down the whole length of the runway, dropped a few degrees of flap and opened up. The wheels rotated about three turns and the Storch soared upwards. Sucking in the flaps, I trundled off to Le Kef and delivered it to a delighted Commander-in-Chief.

With the promise of two more Storches, I mentioned the 190 and the 109's to 'Mary' Coningham.[1] He gave me authority to try and get them to La Marsa. They could then be shipped to the UK for comparative trials with Allied aircraft. This was easier said than done, and my first problem arose with the collection of the Focke-Wulf 190 from Sidi Ahmad airfield at Biserte. I had two RAF Commandos with me and we checked the engine and airframe for any obvious faults. We painted red, white and blue

---

[1] The nickname 'Mary' derived from 'Maori', the Air Marshal being a New Zealander.

tricolours over the swastikas and I took a final cockpit familiarization check. An American army lieutenant-colonel, dressed like Action Man, wandered over and demanded what in tarnation I thought I was doing. I told him I had authority from the C-in-C to take the 190 and was about to do so.

'Like hell you are!' he snarled, precipitating a heated argument over the rightful ownership of the aircraft. He belaboured me with his self-importance as deputy base commander and CO of the local US anti-aircraft unit, stressing dramatically that if I attempted to take off he would order his men to shoot me down.

I sized him up as having a zero IQ at birth which in the passage of some forty-five summers had shown no significant improvement. Having delivered his ultimatum he gumshoed away as the midday meal gong sounded. GI's appeared from all directions heading for the field kitchen, and I seized my chance. My two erks cranked the inertia starter and the engine fired up. I held it at a fast tick over until the oil temperature registered, then taxied out. Trundling along the ramp I passed the long chow line, headed of course by the colonel still wearing his ridiculous tin hat. I flipped two lazy fingers at him in a farewell gesture, and gunned away on the take-off.

The 190 handled beautifully, and had an impressive all-round visibility from the cockpit. However, despite several re-cycles I couldn't get the starboard gear to retract, so keeping the speed below 200-kph, I made my way to La Marsa. A swarm of RAF Commandos descended on my steed and rapidly isolated the retraction problem which was traced to a frayed wire electrical fault.

The Me 109F had been located on a strip near Cap Bon and was in good shape. Safely displaced from interruption by obtuse colonels, we took our time over inspection of the Messerschmitt which paid dividends. On take-off and in the initial climb it handled very like a Spitfire. It was, however, fitted with wing slots which popped out at unexpected moments inducing a skid which threw the aircraft's true attitude momentarily off line. The heavy flat-sided canopy seemed to have more metal than perspex, and cockpit visibility was infinitely worse than a Spitfire. Nevertheless, I enjoyed the jaunt to La Marsa, and remember thinking that if I'd flown the

109 earlier in the war, I wouldn't have been half so impressed with its reputation.

Collecting the Me 109G from La Sebela was fraught with incident. On engine run-ups the radiator temperature registered a high reading albeit a steady one. Eventually I took off and stayed within reach of the field in case of emergency, but the gauge still read high. After landing the fitters had another careful look at the cooling system, but nothing untoward emerged. I took off again for a dash to La Marsa, but on reaching about 1,000-feet dire noises clanked from the engine as it seized to a stop. Fortunately there were flat open spaces dead ahead and I bellied down. It was good-bye to the 109 for which I refuted some wag's suggestion to add to my score and claim as destroyed.

After much dedicated work by the Commandos, the Me 109F and the Fw 190 motored sweetly, and it was an enjoyable experience for me to perform a number of air tests. Both aircraft had a high performance for their day, and of the two I much preferred the Focke-Wulf.

In July 1943 the Allies invaded Sicily without undue difficulty. The North West African Air Force was expanded to become the 1st Allied Tactical Air Force commanded by Sir Arthur Coningham and the headquarters was set up at Cassibile just south of Syracuse. I was posted to the emporium on the staff of Ronnie Lees who became Group Captain Operations.

My duties consisted of coordinating army requests for air support. The hub of this activity stemmed from a caravan manned by myself and two army majors by names of Jack Profumo and John Haire, both destined to be Conservative MP's in post-war parliament. These two worthies were most efficient, and were blessed with a sense of humour which unfailingly led to hilarious situations on aspects which could otherwise prove to be boringly mundane. The day's work was invariably completed by breakfast-time, and after that we were free to pursue other activities which we fondly believed would enhance the progress of the war.

A mixed fluid and static state existed in Sicily for several weeks as the Allies sought to push the Axis back to the mainland of Italy. In the north General Patton's II Corps steamed round the island to threaten the Messina strait, while Montgomery came to his familiar full stop on the

Lentini plain south of Catania. Communications, as ever in an Allied overseas theatre, were deplorably unreliable. To ensure certain dispatches were received and answered by the scattered Allied commanders, I was increasingly employed as a flying courier and had my own Spitfire V allotted for the purpose. I duly delivered the missives to the staffs of Generals Eisenhower, Montgomery and Patton, along with the Air Officers Commanding Malta, Africa and the Desert Air Force.

In the midst of one of my courier trips one day, I landed at the Air Headquarters strip near Hammamet in Tunisia. I fell prey to the usual interminable delay in the arrival of transport to convey me to my destination. It has always been quite extraordinary how the Royal Air Force can supply aircraft to cover some four hundred miles in about an hour and take twice the time to provide conveyance over the last few miles.

Standing alone by the sandy strip, I watched a Lockhead Hudson arrive, and as it taxied in, a rank pennant fluttered above the cockpit. It denoted the highest rank aboard as being a Marshal of the Royal Air Force. The aircraft stopped near me in a cloud of dust and as the rear door opened, a ladder was lowered and down stepped a tall, angular senior officer whom I recognised as Lord Trenchard. I looked anxiously round for some welcoming party but the airfield was barren.

The old gentleman, then in his seventy-first year, unconcernedly parked his backside on a shooting stick, and calmly awaited events. I stepped forward a couple of paces and threw him a salute of which even Cranwell would have approved. Not for nothing was he nicknamed 'Boom' as his voice reverberated across the field.

'Come here, boy,' he demanded, and as I moved over he asked, 'What's your name, boy?'

'Oxspring, sir,' I said.

'Hum,' he reflected. 'Did you have a father in the Royal Flying Corps?'

'Yes, sir,' I replied.

'Ah,' he recalled. "Fifty-four Squadron, St Omer 1917!'

As I assured him that he was quite correct, a convoy of cars belted on to the strip in a cloud of dust and disgorged panic-stricken brass all gushing profuse apologies for their late arrival. Graciously his Lordship insisted on a seat for me in his car, and chatted pleasantly about my father throughout the ride to the mess. I had a short but impressive insight to the qualities that had made him not only the father of the RAF, but all other air forces of the world to follow.

As the Allies consolidated, certain senior officers at headquarters prowled around with hot files and worried expressions. Eventually the secret was revealed. I was briefed by the American Deputy Commander, General 'Uncle Joe' Cannon that the Italian government was making overtures for a cessation of hostilities. It was expected that a mission consisting of Marshal Badoglio and his government ministers would fly from Rome the following day to discuss armistice terms with General Eisenhower. The air force's part in this operation was to ensure the safe arrival of the Roman backsides at Palermo. Arrangements were that the Savoia aircraft transporting the mission would be escorted half way across the Mediterranean by Italian fighters, and the rest of the way by our own.

Uncle Joe told me that the squadron selected to perform the task was the 99th 'Pursuit' based near Termini on a northern coastal strip. My duty was to brief the squadron to conduct the escort without revealing to the pilots the significance of the flight, and to stress that on no account were they to endanger the Savoia or mix it with the Italian escort.

I took off next morning and landed at first light. The 99th was an all-negro P40 Warhawk Squadron commanded by a stalwart ex-West Pointer, Major Davis. He assembled his pilots on the beach by the strip and as darkness faded, I faced a spectre of gleaming white eyeballs and shining teeth. I unfolded the operation emphasising the need for security. The 99th completed the task impeccably, and the following day Italy was out of the war.

American pilots established a reputation for expressive speech on inter-flight radio calls, and none more so than the coloured boys of the 99th 'Pursuit'.

During the Salerno landing, in which the Allied armies attempted to leapfrog up the Italian coast towards Rome, the 99th, in concert with other Allied fighter squadrons, was allocated its specific patrols over the beachhead. Penetrating a bit too far over the enemy defenses, the 99th were subjected to their first taste of the venomous German 88-mm flak.

Shellbursts exploded in and around the squadron with an intensity that split the formation. The squadron commander moved seawards and anxiously called instructions to reassemble his outfit. In the midst of the confusion a dialogue hit the ether:

Say, boss, this is yo' Red fo; mah engine's runnin' real rough. I figure I'll RTB.'[2]

'Red fo', this is yo' boss; you'se jes' as shit scared as the rest of us; yo' tuck yo' ass back in fo'mation, pronto.'

Followed by:

'Say, boss, blue one heah, one Bandit five o'clock low –'

'Say you, guys. I'se no Bandit. I'sejes' lost.'

Out of the blue came a letter from home announcing my father's sudden death from a heart attack. Since my personal inputs did not appear to be noticeably affecting the course of the war, I successfully applied for compassionate leave. Armed with travel orders I hitch-hiked an uncomfortable ride in a USAAF B26 to Gibraltar, and thence by B17 Fortress to England.

Before my leave expired, an order arrived cancelling my return to Sicily but instead to report to Fighter Command at Stanmore. A vacant slot needed filling in the Tactics and Training branch of the illustrious headquarters, and I joined a formidable squad of fellow tour-expired veterans whose cavalier approach to their work sent spasms of horror through the dedicated Staff College graduates. The tactics and training publications directed at the day fighter squadrons were entrusted to three of us sharing an office.

Jackie Urwin-Mann, a prewar vintage Canadian who had sweated through the Battle of Britain and the Western Desert, occupied one chair. The third desk was the domain of Pat Lardner-Burke, a rugged South African who, with Hornchurch sweeps and Malta behind him, displayed a refreshingly irreverent attitude to all senior officers with whom he disagreed.[2] Facetious comments filled the minute sheets of numerous files which we solemnly circulated between ourselves, and on rare occasions to other departments. Delaying as long as possible any publication from Fighter Command on our particular subjects, our natures rebelled at the

---

1 RTB. Return to Base.
2 Spitfire Mark IX No MH434 with which Pat shot down two Fw 190's plus a shared and a damaged when flying with 222 Squadron from Hornchurch in 1943 was, over forty years later, often seen at air displays all over Europe being superbly flown by Ray Hannah, the first Red Arrows' leader.

preposterous notion of issuing a training directive to the likes of Johnnie Johnson, or a tactics manual to Sailor Malan.

The monotony was shattered one afternoon by the sudden arrival of Air Commodore Richard Atcherley, from the newly formed Allied Expeditionary Air Force headquarters. This forum was housed in a massive turreted stone house near Stanmore which he referred to as 'Gremlin Castle'. Batchy, as he was known to all, was the doyen of all fighter pilots. A member of the victorious Schneider Trophy team of 1931 he, along with his twin brother David, was dedicated to the well-being of the Air Force, and their example inspired their fledglings to great achievements. Batchy bounced into our office, preceded by a huge, tongue-lolling Great Dane which, anxious to prove its affection, put a large paw on my flimsy desk and shoved it over.

'Wot cheer, chaps,' quoth Batchy. 'Where's everyone bogged off to?'

He was referring to our immediate seniors whose vacant offices indicated either attendance at an important meeting, or more likely not yet back from lunch.

Undeterred by the absence of more heavy rank than three squadron leaders, Batchy unloaded his problem. With the impending invasion of Europe only a few months ahead, he felt there was a serious discrepancy in the operational knowledge of the fighter squadrons based on UK. None had experience of close support of the Army as recently had been undergone in the Western Desert and Tunisia. He proposed to set up a crash training programme for all wing and squadron leaders in the arts of bombing and rocketry, and had already acquired the use of an airfield at Milfield in Northumberland with access to an extensive weapons' range. His current deficiency was lack of targets at which to launch his bombs and rockets, but had persuaded the Army authorities that it was in their interest to supply them. The problem was that some fifty obsolete tanks and a further hundred worn-out vehicles were all on Salisbury Plain and needed to be on the range some three hundred miles away within a week.

'Get a train to move them, Bobby,' he commanded.

Not being in the business of ordering whole trains at a moment's notice, I didn't quite know where to start, but anything was possible with Batchy behind it. In fact it was surprisingly easy. No doubt the railway authorities took the view that anyone wanting trains comprising some sixty freight cars couldn't be kidding. The whole operation was under way inside 48 hours, but for some days I worried about possible repercussions. My concern was unnecessary. Some years later Batchy confided to me:

'If you're convinced the Air Force wants something badly enough, go ahead and get it; but in case you're court-martialled, make it so expensive you couldn't possibly pay for it!'

March 1944 brought promotion. I was posted back on operations as wing leader of No 24 Wing. The Normandy invasion was three months away.

CHAPTER FOURTEEN

'IF I DON'T GET LEAVE SOON'

'Sir, if I don't get leave soon, my balls 'll burst!'

Warrant Officer Red Bloomer Royal Australian Air Force

Nos 91 and 322 Squadrons comprised the day fighter element of 24 Wing in the 2nd Tactical Air Force. 91, my old friends from Hawkinge, had shed their reconnaissance duties and 322 was the only Netherlands fighter squadron attached to the Royal Air Force. A Mosquito squadron took on the night fighter task and a mobile radar control completed the set-up.

With the imminence of the Allied invasion, 24 Wing's task was to shield the ports and airfields in southern England from enemy air intrusion, particularly high flying reconnaissance flights. In ensuring a maximum interception capability, availability of the top fighter performance was paramount. 91 and 322 Squadrons were accordingly equipped with the Spitfire Mark XIV, the most powerful thoroughbred yet to emerge from the Supermarine stable. Such was the plan which, due to unforeseen circumstances, was to change drastically.

The first priority was to get the pilots fully at home with the Spit XIV which differed considerably from previous Marks of Spitfire in that it was powered by a new Rolls Royce engine, the Griffon Mark IV. To absorb the 2,035 horse-power, the Griffon required a five bladed Rotol propeller which rotated clockwise in the opposite direction to the Merlin. This considerable increase in power coupled with excessive torque, needed the most gentle handling on take-off. No more than two-thirds throttle was required to get the aircraft off the ground.

In converting to the Spit XIV, pilots who appreciated the radical differences from the Mark IX coped quite easily, but those who relaxed or were careless caused some hair-raising incidents. One pilot in particular, Warrant Officer Red Bloomer, who had recently been shot down in France and returned to 91 Squadron after evading capture, was so anxious to get airborne again that he took off in a XIV without adequate briefing. The aircraft leapt off with a gigantic swing which with full rudder he could not hold, then headed at a right angle from the runway towards the hangars. After his wheels missed the top of the buildings by inches, it took those of us who witnessed his hairy exhibition a considerable time to get our toes unknotted.

Some six weeks before the invasion the squadrons deployed to their D-day bases. 91 settled in at West Malling and 322 at Hartford Bridge. An air of subdued tension pervaded the whole country as the mightiest military armada ever assembled took up departure points for D-day. Many thousands of Allied troops and their equipment in the vast military inventory moved to southern England. As some wag put it, 'If the *Luftwaffe* clobber the barrage balloons, Britain will sink.'

Working up the wing to peak efficiency we flew several sweeps to Reims, Rouen, Paris, Brussels and Rotterdam. We were keen to try out our fast-flying XIV's, but to our disappointment the *Luftwaffe* deigned not to be enticed into combat.

On 4th June, 1944, all group captains and wing leaders of the fighter task force were summoned to Tangmere. I flew down with Wing Commander Windy Reid, CO of the Canadian night fighter squadron at West Malling, in his Mosquito. The invasion, codenamed '*Overlord*', was scheduled for the following day and an impressive briefing took two hours to complete. The Form D operations order which rolled off the teleprinter was 28-feet long, and its complexity was breathtaking. On return to West Malling the Station Commander met us with the news that because of rough weather

Overload was postponed for twenty-four hours. We could not therefore divulge our information to anyone. With our trip to Tangmere having been noted, it was not easy to keep sealed lips from the curious types anxiously soliciting 'pukka gen'.

Very few of us on the wing had much sleep that night. 322 Squadron were informed that Prince Bernhard of the Netherlands intended to fly in early on D-day. His visits were always most popular events not only with the Dutch boys but everybody else. His personality and optimistic enthusiasm had an inspiring quality. Coincidentally, a message reached me from very high altitude down the RAF chain that an exceedingly dim view would be taken if, as suspected, Prince Bernhard endeavoured to fly over the invasion zone.

He arrived at Hartford Bridge an hour after dawn and precipitated no little excitement by unfortunately bursting a tyre on landing. He was indeed desperately keen to climb into a Spit XIV in order to cross the Channel and witness the epic assault on the Normandy beaches. It was an invidious situation to have to try and dissuade him, especially when 322's Spitfire XIV's belonged to his London-based Netherlands government. In the event, the Prince appreciated the embarrassing position I was in, and after a couple of hours he returned to London no doubt with the intention of expressing his vexation in high circles.

The wing's mission from D-day onwards was to intercept any reconnaissance or bombing missions the *Luftwaffe* might mount against the southern English ports and airfields. Strangely, practically nothing ventured that far, and the temptation to see how the invasion was getting on without our help was too much. Two of us set course at 35,000-feet from the Isle of Wight along the string of ships as they sailed several lines deep across the Channel. Activity at the bridgeheads was intense, with innumerable small craft ploughing back and forth to the mother vessels. Dense clouds of smoke poured from destroyers laying screens around the main fleet as explosions erupted inland signifying intense battles in progress with the enemy. Above all, swarms of Allied aircraft were either patrolling or heading across the coast on tactical strikes. It was a spectacle the like of which could never be repeated.

During the eventful days which followed I renewed acquaintance with

George Keefer. After three years overseas George had an opportunity to take a short, well-earned leave at home in Canada, and on return was due to take over No 125 wing in France as wing leader. He had a four-legged problem. His inseparable companion was a magnificent German shepherd alsatian, just fully grown, which appropriately answered to the name of Rommel. Since he could not take Rommel with him on his forthcoming travels, George was looking for someone to look after him and I volunteered. About half a dozen pilots rendezvous'd at the Grand Hotel in Brighton for the handing over ceremony and after a few beers at the bar we trooped off to the dining room where we ran into a Fawlty Towers situation. The head waiter barred the entrance to George stating:

'You can't bring that animal in here, sir.'

'You try and put him out,' was the succinct response.

Rommel was admitted.

After savage fighting for footholds in Normandy the Allied armies established bridgeheads and advanced inland. The Americans led by Bradley and Patton moved south and west to isolate the Cherbourg peninsula.

The British and Canadian armies commanded by Montgomery battled through some heavy fighting for some ten miles before coming to a full stop at Caen. Four Panzer divisions, three of them manned by SS troops, arrested their progress. To help him get moving again, Monty demanded RAF strikes on the Panzers not only from the 2nd Tactical Air Force but from Bomber Command as well. The protestations of the C-in-C, Sir Arthur Harris, that such an operation was a gross misuse of his strategic force were overruled, and in consequence over 700 heavy bombers were scheduled to carpet-bomb the Panzer dispositions in the vicinity of Caen. 24 Wing's part in the operation was target cover; normally Bomber Command only operated at night, but on this occasion the stream of Lancasters and Halifaxes took advantage of a bright, sunny day.

From 20,000-feet the cleverly camouflaged Panzer divisions were nowhere in evidence, but the Pathfinder bomb aimers cascaded their marker flares down on a map co-ordinate. The rest of the force solemnly followed on and rained several thousand tons of high explosive on the markers which, inside half an hour, effectively reduced several square miles of France to dust. Although the Panzers were considerably shaken by the bombardment, their fighting efficiency was not substantially reduced. Conversely, when the British and Canadians attacked shortly afterwards, their advance was severely hampered by a moon surface of large bomb craters. Sir Arthur Harris was right; employment of strategic forces in a tactical role was inexpedient. The steamroller found a nut hard to crack.

One week after D-day, Hitler launched his V1 weapons on London. Whilst not entirely unexpected, the intensive assault of flying bombs caught the British air defence system in disarray. Tabbed as 'Doodlebugs' by the public, Fighter Command allocated the code name 'Diver' for defensive operations to counter the threat. Stationed as we were with our high performance Spit XIV's at West Malling, we were ideally placed to react to the continuous stream of missiles from their launch sites in the Pas de Calais. Mounting standing patrols, we and the newly formed high-speed Tempest wing led by Wing Commander Roly Beamont were controlled for interceptions by Biggin Hill operations. Unfortunately our initial efforts were often handicapped by an onrush of miscellaneous aircraft from all over the country whose pilots were out to get themselves a Doodlebug. These chaps ranged from elderly staff officers to young pilots who had just joined a squadron. All were strapped to lethal fighters, and none were under operational control of Biggin Hill or anyone else. We dubbed these guys the 'Wolf Pack', and when attacking our targets spent anxious moments dodging streams of lead as they hose-piped at ranges of 2,000-yards or more.

Until we gained a little experience, the art of destroying Doodlebugs caused us much chagrin and sometimes grief. The average speed of the targets was 400-mph which was around the low level limits of the Spit XIV's and Tempests. It was necessary to maintain a high cruising speed and superior altitude to be able to drop on the Divers as they streaked across Kent towards London. My first encounter occurred at Maidstone, and as I curved after my target I underestimated its speed and found myself in a stern chase. Very slowly I reduced the range until able to fire, and as I did so bits flew off the rear end and the craft plummeted down. Concentrating on the action I had not kept track of my position until I saw to my consternation my target explode on a Nissen hut in the bounds of Battersea power station. The hut disintegrated but I afterwards heard to my relief that there were no casualties.

Sir Roderic Hill, Air Marshal Commanding, Air Defence Great Britain, soon got the defenses geared to the threat. Barrage balloons from all over UK were packed in depth around south-east London. British and American anti-aircraft units using promixity fused shells concentrated along the south coast in the narrow Channel area. All forms of wolf pack were forbidden and two fighter intercept zones were allocated; one out to sea in the Channel, and the other inland between the gunbelt and the balloons.

We found the ideal tactics for destroying these menacing missiles to be crucially governed by the range at which we fired. Over 250-yards usually hit the flying control system of the craft which would dive to the ground still with an active warhead. Often a range of 150-yards or less almost always clobbered the warhead which could severely damage the attacking fighter. The ultimate lay in accurate shooting between 200 and 250-yards which provided a reasonable certainty of exploding the warhead in the air without undue danger to the fighter.

Not surprisingly, the standard of shooting by the squadrons deployed against the Divers improved to a very high standard. An outstanding personal score of sixty-one destroyed was credited to Squadron Leader J Berry, CO of No 3 Squadron flying Tempests. No less than twenty-two pilots achieved scores of between fifteen and forty apiece. Our ace on 24 Wing was Dutchman Rudi Burgwal of 322 Squadron who, in a total of twenty-one, demolished five in one sortie.

Conversely, the pilotless Buzz bomb could turn round and bite. In a chase over southern Kent, French pilot Capitaine Jean Maridor of 91 Squadron fired and hit a target in the tail control causing it to dive. To his consternation he saw it falling directly on a military field hospital identified by a large red cross in the grounds. Many witnesses testified that the gallant Frenchman, not having time to set up another firing attack, deliberately rammed the warhead which exploded and killed him.

Shortly afterwards, Flight Lieutenant 'Gin' Seagers, a Belgian attached to the same squadron, lost his life within sight of the airfield when he attacked a target from an awkward angle of fully 90°. Trying to pull enough deflection he lost sight of it under his nose and misjudged his distance. To our horror he struck the warhead which in a deadly flash demolished both target and Spitfire.

The speed of the Spit XIV was a vital adjunct to the defence requirements against the Diver assault on London, and the original plan for 24 Wing to move to Normandy in D plus 30 days was shelved. Consequently our immediate future was geared to the length of the V1 threat which could only be eliminated when the Allied advance through France and Belgium overran the launching sites.

The regularity of the anti-Diver patrols meant that we could schedule flights well ahead and we were able to enjoy some daylight hours off duty. Rommel and I took every advantage afforded us. One beautiful summer afternoon we made tracks for an inviting swimming pool at the Hilden Manor club near Tonbridge. I dived into water and surfaced to see a frantic, barking Rommel circling the pool at high speed. Each time I tried to climb out he threatened to come in on top of me. Finally Kyn Kynaston grabbed the near hysterical dog and as I neared the side I pleaded with Kyn to hold him back. Unfortunately Kyn couldn't resist the temptation for some fun and released him. Rommel arrived on top of me and his flailing claws ripped ribbons of flesh from my body and thighs, I held his throat at arm's length to keep away the snapping jaws trying to grab me in a rescue attempt. With the help of everybody around we finally gained dry land and Rommel relaxed.

'That,' commented Kyn, 'is a one man dog.'

A few weeks afterwards George arrived back to reclaim his pet. Rommel was ecstatic, bounding at George in a joyful reunion. Later they left, and as I watched them depart Rommel's eyes were on George with never a backward look. He was indeed a one man dog. It was a sunny day, but for the first time in two months I no longer had a shadow.

CHAPTER FIFTEEN

'A Couple of Chattering Wrecks'

Wing Commander Pat Lardner-Burke DFC

Returning to West Malling from a trip to Yorkshire one day, I had to contend with some poor weather in the London area. Cloud base was around 1,000-feet and visibility in a thick haze only a few hundred yards. I headed for a mile wide corridor through the balloon barrage across the Thames from Tilbury to Gravesend. The dreaded balloons lurked in the clouds with their cables forming an invisible barrier on a sixty-mile front across south and east London. I concentrated on my map reading to ensure that I was dead on track for the centre of the corridor.

Arriving over Tilbury, I headed for Gravesend which I could barely distinguish across the river. Halfway over the stick jumped violently in my hand and my Spit banked suddenly to the left. Thinking I'd fouled a cable I shat bricks until I found the aircraft still flying. It turned to port and I could not crank enough starboard aileron to straighten out. Peering at the right wing I spied a large jagged hole in the metal aileron which was jammed in a slightly down position. Throttling back and winding on trim, I assumed a more conventional attitude but the Spit continued to turn. In a series of gigantic circles to the left I headed along the north shore of the Thames estuary, sweating blood at the proximity of unseen cables, until I saw Southend airfield. Dropping the gear I somehow managed to keep the port wing up with judicious use of right rudder and landed with a sigh of relief.

The damage had been caused by a strike from a Bofors-type anti-aircraft shell. After searching enquiries through North Weald Ops it was established that it had been fired from a navy supply ship on the Thames underneath. The captain was a hairy old salt of the Royal Navy Reserve who, despite stringent regulations on opening fire in friendly waters, had been bombed at Dunkirk and had sworn that no aircraft would ever fly over his ship again. God bless the Senior Service.

Two months after D-day, the Allied armies broke through the German containment in Normandy and advanced at high speed through north-east France towards Belgium and Holland. The days of the V1 launching sites were numbered. Fighter Command and the 2nd Tactical Air Force rapidly redeployed their fighter squadrons which had been held back in the UK to counter the Diver menace.

The Dutch 322 Squadron, anxious to be in the van of the liberation of Holland, moved quickly to France. 91 Squadron, much to their chagrin, handed over their Spit XIV's to Colin Gray's 2nd TAF Wing and were rearmed again with Spit IX's. As the day fighter element of 24 Wing had become disbanded, my own posting was switched to wing leader of No 141 Wing at Deanland.

As the British and Canadian armies advanced speedily into the Low Countries, our temporary task was the escort of 2nd TAF bombers to tactical targets. Little was seen of the *Luftwaffe*, which since D-day had been overwhelmed by the massive superiority of the Allied air forces.

The latter days of September kept us fully occupied escorting the gallant airborne troops to the debacle at Arnhem. Tasked with seizing and holding key bridges over the Rhine at Arnhem and the Waal at Nijmegen, the British and American Airborne Brigades, according to plan, were to be relieved within 48-hours by Monty's 2nd Army.

Some of us had escorted airborne drops before in Tunisia where little hostile activity had been encountered, but Arnhem was very different. Pitifully poor intelligence prior to the operation had not elucidated the fact that a fully operational Panzer division was in the Arnhem area at the lime. The writing was on the wall before the drops were made.

Weaving over the train of C-47 Dakota tugs, we escorted the first wave of gliderborne troops to the drop zone at Arnhem. It was a spectacular sight as the Horsa gliders rammed the deck from all angles, some breaking up in collisions with trees or other obstacles, and indeed with each other. We had to admire the airborne boys; what a way to get pitched into combat.

Our next protégés were the paratroops. Streams of Dakotas flying in vics of three discharged their cargoes, and banks of multi-coloured parachutes floated passively down. Successive missions saw the German flak get more intense. A number of the slow-flying Daks suffered direct hits and fell like flaming torches with their helpless occupants still aboard.

Three days passed and the tension mounted. Para reinforcements and fresh supplies were hurled into the inferno which Arnhem had become. No information reached us as to how the battle fared. In hindsight we know that Montgomery's 2nd Army failed to relieve the gallant Airbornes in the scheduled forty-eight hours; indeed never did so at all.

For nearly two weeks the heroic lightly-armed Red Devils fought tenaciously against vastly superior German armour and artillery. With radio communications practically non-existent, their hopes that 2nd Army would break through the enemy cordon at any hour spurred their defiance. Each day the Dakotas of RAF and US Transport Commands streamed in with ammunition and rations. Unfortunately the lack of contact with the troops resulted in the cargoes being delivered to some drop zones which had been overrun, and a great preponderance of the urgently needed supplies fell into enemy hands.

To add to the difficulties of the Arnhem and Nijmegen adventures, the weather was poor and severely hampered the desperate air endeavours to help the beleagured troops. At the height of the conflict fog enshrouded much of eastern England and prohibited take off of considerable elements of the re-supply force, particularly the escorting fighters. The 21st September was a particularly bad day. We in 141 Wing based at Manston managed to get airborne for our task of cover to the Dakota train over a turning point at Eindhoven. American P47 Thunderbolt fighters were responsible for cover at the drop zone at Arnhem, but unknown to us the weather in England had prevented them taking off. We duly rendezvous'd with our Dakota charges at Eindhoven and watched them stream into the German flak around Arnhem some forty miles away.

Seeing no other Allied fighters in the area, we followed the Dak train. Way ahead hundreds of parachutes billowed down as the Dakotas wheeled away, and flickers of sunlight winked from what we mistakenly took to be Thunderbolt cover. Suddenly a couple of Daks exploded in fireballs and the stark truth struck us as we eyeballed a number of fighters peeling out of attacks. We poured on the coals and roared in on a dozen Fw 190's as they started to wreak carnage among the defenceless Daks. Before we could engage, the Focke-Wulfs refused a fight and took off eastwards at high speed. We hung around until the last Dakotas completed their drops and dutifully covered the withdrawal. No one could have tried harder to ease the plight of the Red Devils than the dedicated crews of the transports. Our admiration was absolute.

The *Luftwaffe* fighter squadrons were being rapidly decimated by the overwhelming Allied air supremacy, and had mostly withdrawn within the borders of Germany. Resistance to the western strategic bomber onslaught had weakened to a point where Bomber Command considered it prudent to switch most of its offensive from night operations to daylight. Accordingly, the Fighter Command squadrons were allocated for escort duty. No 141 Wing was disbanded, and my next assignment was as Wing Leader of the Detling wing. This outfit comprised No 1 Squadron, pugnaciously led by South African Pat Lardner-Burke, together with No 165 Squadron, commanded by the unflappable Jas Storrar who had knocked up a formidable score of kills since the outbreak of war.

Our biggest problem in escorting Bomber Command was the limited range of the Spitfire. A partial solution was to carry jettisonable external tanks mounted under the fuselage with capacities of either 45 or 90-gallons of fuel. The former increased endurance to about three hours, but the 90 gallon mode was a ferry type configuration which reduced the aircraft's performance to a barely acceptable level. The obvious remedy was to install an internal fuselage tank behind the pilot as the Americans had achieved with the P51 Mustang, but flight tests disclosed that with a similar modification the Spitfire's centre of gravity shifted aft to a dangerous degree.

Our range capability was dramatically increased when Fighter Command set up airstrips at Maldegem and Ursel in the Gent area of Belgium. From these two bases we were able to cover most of the strategic targets in western Germany which Bomber Command had scheduled for demolition.

The offensive got under way and we were treated to the awesome sight of Bomber Command at work. Efficient as the heavy boys were, they seemed incapable of flying neat, tidy formations which would have made our task of escorting them so much easier. As it was, some bomber squadrons made half-hearted attempts to close up the space, but most merely adapted night tactics to daylight, resulting in a gigantic stream of four engined aircraft stretching some sixty miles long. This posed a problem for us to cover the vulnerable flanks, and usually the entire resources of Fighter Command were required to protect a single raid.

The strength of the operations varied depending on the priority of the targets. Any number between 400 and 900 heavies could comprise a raid with equal forces of fighters giving cover. Innumerable dense contrails stretched from the UK to Germany tracing the path of the onslaught. Ribbons of 'Window'[1] twinkled beneath the gaggle as the crews shovelled out heaps of foil to confuse the enemy radars.

Operations against German industrial targets were as frequent as weather conditions of the 1944/45 winter would allow. Isolated long range targets such as Bayreuth and Munich were rare, and the intensity was concentrated on the Ruhr, or 'Happy Valley' as it was flippantly known. Shortage of pilots and aviation fuel severely curtailed the *Luftwaffe's* capacity to oppose the strategic intrusions. Lack of resistance did not, however, apply to the flak units of the Wehrmacht, particularly in the industrial heartland of the Ruhr. Penetration to the more easterly targets such as Dortmund called for a 50-mile gauntlet run through accurate heavy flak, dense enough as the bomber crews declared 'to put down the undercart and taxi home on it!' Flying several thousand feet above our charges we fighters with our constant manoeuvrings were not specifically targeted. But it was inspiring to witness the guts of the bomber crews as, concentrating on their bombing runs, they drove undeviatingly into the

---

[1] Strips of metal foil which in quantity fogged the reflection;, to enemy radar screens. Known lo the Americans as 'Chaff'.

lethal defensive curtain.

Nor was the flak inaccurate. All too frequently one of the heavies would be stricken by a direct hit. Sometimes the hapless bomber would erupt in an instantaneous explosion, but more often some vital part of engines or airframe ceased to function. As it lost station and altitude we would wait breathlessly to count the parachutes of the crews baling out, but often none would emerge and we'd watch the sickening sight of the fatal plunge.

With bombs still aboard as it approached a target near Hannover one day, a Halifax dropped out of the stream obviously in trouble. Seven chutes bloomed as the crew baled out, after which the huge bomber fell into a near vertical dive. Some thousands of feet lower the trim forces took effect and it wallowed into a climb completing a perfect loop followed by no less than two more before hitting the deck. It was an epic example of the strength of the Halifax's construction; how the wings stayed on under such enormous stress I'll never know.

Aiming on the Pathfinder markers the main force released their high explosive 'Cookies' which on impact shed rings of blast waves which could be clearly seen from 25,000-feet. At the same time canisters of countless incendiaries were released which, if there was any wind to fan them, reduced the targets to raging infernos.

A couple of weeks before Christmas 1944, we escorted the heavies in an attack on an ammunition dump at Heimbach and landed at Brussels to top up with fuel before returning to UK. By the time we set course for Manston it was late afternoon and dusk was upon us. Crossing out near Ostend, low cloud and fog patches gathered over the North Sea and we switched on navigation lights for the wing to keep formation.

Only a couple of days previously the final installation of 'Fido' had been completed at Manston and the Station Commander was keyed up for an excuse to turn it on. Fido was a fog dispersal equipment burning contaminated petrol which provided intense heat down the sides of the runway thereby lifting the precipitation upwards by several hundred feet. As we pointed into the ever darkening gloom, the Station Commander called me asking if we would like the assistance of Fido. I readily agreed and a few minutes later the sky ahead lit up in a magic glow as Manston's Fido flared up, burning at the rate of a million gallons an hour. Fido was expensive, but was one of the great inventions of the war and fulfilled Winston Churchill's decree that 'Fog will be dispersed'. Our twenty-four Spitfires settled down safely as did countless battle-damaged aircraft caught out by weather in the later stages of the war.

Next morning the wing lined up on Manston's vast runway for return to home base at Detling. Leading No 1 Squadron, I had almost gained flying speed when my engine cut dead. Holding rudder against the torque I couldn't prevent a violent swing across the path of Pat Lardner-Burke formating on my wing. Pat hauled back on his stick and his aircraft literally jumped over the top of me. I can still visualize every single rivet on his under fuselage as he careered over my canopy. Bouncing down off his kangaroo leap, he demanded:

'What the hell goes on, Bobby?'

The wing roared away as I trundled off the runway with a fuel starvation problem; I didn't need to remove my helmet, my hair shot up so straight it just pushed it off. Pat's lightning reactions avoided a messy pile up. Years afterwards we still chilled over the memory. Such dramas tend to play hell with the nervous system. As Pat remarked, 'Man, we bloody near became a couple of chattering wrecks.'

In a despairing show of defiance to a raid on Essen, the *Luftwaffe* pumped up a pair of Me 262's high above the bomber stream. It was the first time we'd seen the much vaunted German jets. We jettisoned our external tanks and prepared for battle but they declined to engage and disappeared at high speed. The final glimpse I had of the *Luftwaffe* was a solitary Messerschmitt 163 rocket-powered delta fighter which, leaving a long black trail, climbed at astonishing speed into a formation of Lancasters. Before we could cut it off', it fired but missed, and creamed away into the stratosphere, not to be seen again.

The British and American armies crossed the Rhine and were poised to reach forward to Germany's eastern frontier. Unfortunately the ailing President Roosevelt would not authorise further progress until the Russians had a chance to be in at the kill. For a frustrating few weeks the western Allies marked time whilst the Red Army pillaged and raped its barbarous progress through eastern Europe. Admirable as was the Soviets' ferocious defence of their homeland, as steadfast allies they were a dead loss. Throughout the wartime confrontation Russia constantly demanded war materials which Britain at least could ill afford. Vital supplies were sent to their aid, but not once did they offer to help transport them. Many ships were lost and numberless British seamen died in the ill-fated relief convoys to the Barents Sea, with not a word of gratitude from our so-called comrades in arms. For lack of equipment and know how, no Russian heavy bombardment operations existed to help out the hard-pressed crews of Bomber Command and the US 8th Air Force. Indeed, it was perhaps just as well since the mood of Soviet inconsonance would have boded ill for the highly sophisticated strategic air offensive mounted by the west. With 'friends' like these, who needs enemies?

April 1945 arrived, and the end of the war loomed close. German armed resistance began to collapse and was maintained only in isolated fanatical pockets, particularly in Berlin. Among the garrisons determined to fight to the last were those of Heligoland and Wangcrooge which for years had been thorns in the side of Bomber Command when utilizing the Baltic routes to the German heartland. Both these islands were loaded with searchlight and heavy flak units. Hitherto more urgent priority targets had prevented the heavies from hitting back at their plaguey assailants. On 18th April, Headquarters Bomber Command relented and issued an operational order to 'sink Heligoland'. Halifaxes and Lancasters built up a maximum effort and cratered the island from end to end in a devastating attack. At the height of the raid, half a dozen German high speed launches flushed out in a desperate dash for the sanctity of the mainland, only to run into a hail of cannon fire from our escorting fighters who queued up gleefully to let go with their final fusillades. Even so, Major Werner Christie, CO of 331 Norwegian Squadron, had his Mustang hit by return fire. He baled out and paddled ashore in his dinghy, to the great hilarity of his fellow fighter pilots.

A week later, in the last major air strike of the European war, Wangerooge was subjected to similar treatment to that accorded Heligoland. It was also my operational finale.

My posting awaited to the Central Fighter Establishment at Tangmere. The day before VE Day I strapped on a Spitfire for a carefree sortie of aerobatics. I had reason to celebrate. Notice arrived from the Air Ministry that I'd been granted a permanent commission in the RAF, so my future was secure. I could scarcely believe I was still in one piece after six years of war and still flying my faithful Spitfire. Other pilots whose operations started on Spitfires transferred their allegiance to alternative fighters of excellent wartime design, among them the Typhoon, Mustang and Tempest. Thanks to the dedicated engineers at Supermarine and Rolls Royce, the Spitfire remained Queen of the sky. Circumstances had aligned my embattled survival with her ever increasing performance.

I landed and parked next to a Meteor, the RAF's first operational jet. It was the end of an era. The days of the propeller-driven fighter were over. I looked back at the graceful lines of the Spit as, tail down and nose as ever skywards, she seemed to proclaim:

'I've seen and done it all; now it's your turn!'

APPENDIX I

COMBAT RECORD

Group Captain R W Oxspring DFC★★, AFC

Date	Type	Category	Location
29 Jul 40	$^1/_3$ Heinkel 111	Confirmed Destroyed	North Sea
11 Sep 40	one Heinkel 111	Confirmed Destroyed	Channel
15 Sep 40	one Heinkei 111	Damaged	Kent
15 Sep 40	one Heinkei 111	Damaged	Kent
15 Sep 40	one Dornier 17	Confirmed Destroyed	Rochester
18 Sep 40	one Me 109 E	Confirmed Destroyed	Dover
18 Sep 40	one Me 109 E	Damaged	Hawkinge
24 Sep 40	one Heinkei 111	Confirmed Destroyed	Hastings
27 Sep 40	one Me 110	Confirmed Destroyed	Biggin Hill
27 Sep40	one Dornier 215	Damaged	Kent
30 Sep 40	one Me 109 E	Confirmed Destroyed	Biggin Hill
05 Oct 40	one Me 109 E	Confirmed Destroyed	Chatham
13 Oct 40	one Me 109 E	Confirmed Destroyed	Ashford
26 Jul 42	one Fw 190	Probably Destroyed	Calais
25 Nov 42	one Me 109 F	Damaged	Mateur

Date	Type	Category	Location
25 Nov 42	one Me 109 F	Probably Destroyed	Mateur
26 Nov 42	one Ju 88	Damaged	Djedeida
29 Nov 42	one Macchi 202	Damaged	Djedeida
30 Nov 42	one Savoia 79	Damaged	Tebourba
01 Dec 42	one Macchi 202	Damaged	Tunis
03 Dec 42	one Me 109 F	Damaged	Tebourba
05 Dec 42	one Me 109 F	Confirmed Destroyed	Biserte
22 Dec 42	one Fw 190	Confirmed Destroyed	Owed Zarga
02 Jan 43	one Me 109 F	Confirmed Destroyed	Pont du Fahs
02 Jan 43	one Me 109 F	Damaged	St Cyprien
28 Feb 43	one Fw 190	Damaged	Beja
01 Mar 43	one Me 109 G	Confirmed Destroyed	Beja
11 Apr 43	one Me 109 F	Confirmed Destroyed	Medjez El Bab
11 Apr 43	one Me 109 F	Damaged	Medjez El Bab
08 Jun 42	one French rail locomotive destroyed Eu station		Nr Le Treport
21 Nov 42	four German trucks destroyed in flames		Mateur
22 Nov 42	six German trucks destroyed in flames		Mateur
22 Nov 42	one German staffcar destroyed		Mateur
23 Jun 44	one V1 Diver (Buzz bomb) destroyed		Battersea
29 Jun 44	one V1 Diver (Buzz bomb) destroyed		Nr Tonbridge
06 Jul 44	one V1 Diver (Buzz bomb) destroyed		SW Maidstone
16 Jul 44	one V1 Diver (Buzz bomb) destroyed		S Ashford

APPENDIX II

BIBLIOGRAPHY

Battle Over Britain Francis K Mason, McWhirter Twins 1969

Fighter Command Air Vice-Marshal Peter Wykeham, Putnams 1960

Aces High Christopher Shores and Clive Williams, Neville Spearman 1966

Spitfire – The Story of a Famous Fighter Bruce Robertson, Harleyford 1962

The Greatest Air Battle Norman Franks, William Kimber 1979

Fighter over Tunisia Christopher Shores, Hans Ring, William Hess, Neville Spearman 1975

Spitfire at War Alfred Price, Ian Allan 1974

The Plain Cook and The Great Showman Gregory Blaxland, William Kimber 1977

APPENDIX III

INDEX

Abbeville 85,89
Ajax, HMS 35
Allen, Wg Cdr H R 43, 48, 54, 57, 59. 67
Amiens 15
Andrews, A V M J 92
Appleford, Plt Off A N R L 43
Armstrong, Sqn Ldr H T 90
Arnim, Gen Obst Jurgen Von 105, 124
Arras 15
Atcherley, A M Sir Richard 128, 136

Bader, Gp Cpt Sir Douglas 9 35, 47, 53, 69, 74, 75 93, 120
Badoglio, Marshal 134
Ball VC, Cpt A 14
Bär, Oblt H 72
Barking Creek 32, 33
Barraclough, A G M Sir John 23
Barthropp, Wg Cdr P P C 78
Bartley, Sqn Ldr A C 124, 57, 101
Barwell, Gp Cpt R 78, 86
Beamish, Gp Cpt F V 74, 75, 82, 83, 85
Beamont, Wg Cdr R P 142
Beaumont, Sgt 81-84
Bernhard, H R H Prince 140
Berry, Sqn Ldr J 143
Berry, Gp Cpt R 34, 119

Bertangles 15
Bloomer, W/O 'Red' 138, 139
Bodendiek, Ltn E 57, 58
Bodie, Plt Off C A W 41, 46, 54, 55, 61, 62
Boyd, Gp Cpt R F 82, 83
Brady, Flt Lt 'Jim' 79
Brothers, A Cdre P M 94
Brown, Gp Cpt G A 40
Browne, Sgt F M 111
Browne, Flg Off P S F M 30
Burgwal, Flg Off R 143
Burton, Wg Cdr H F 43, 73, 74

Cameron, Flt Sgt M 59
Campbell-Colquhoun, Wg Cdr EW 40
Cannon, Bg Gen J 134
Chamberlain, Neville 32
Charnock, Flt Lt H W 92, 108
Christie, Flt Lt G P 43
Christie, Maj W 152
Christmas, Flt Lt D 54
Churchill, Sir Winston 17, 38-40, 54, 83, 84, 151
Cobham, Sir Alan 12, 60
Colloredo-Mansfeld, Sqn Ldr F F 91
Coningham, A M Sir Arthur 130, 132
Conrad, Wg Cdr W A G 73

Cooke, Plt Off C A 43
Corbett, Plt Off G H 48, 53, 59, 61
Corbin, Flt Lt W J 92
Cox, Wg Cdr D G S R 104, 106, 113, 120, 121, 125
Craxton, Flg Off C T V 34
Cross, A M Sir Kenneth 37, 128
Daniel, Wg Cdr S W 112, 120

David, Gp Cpt W D 71
Davis, Maj 134
Demozay, Lt Col M 80
Doolittle, Lt Gen J H 115
Douglas, M R A F Sir Wm Sholto 69
Dowding, A C M Lord 8, 38, 41
Drake, Wg Cdr B 78
Dunkirk 38, 39, 146
Dunning-White, Flt Lt P 71
Dunworth, Sqn Ldr F P R 43

Eisenhower, Gen of A Dwight D 133, 134
Esmonde VC. Lt Cdr E 83
Evans, Sgt V 95

Farrish, Flt Lt 119, 125
Flez 15
Forde, Sqn Ldr D 107, 120
Fort Maclaughin, SS 97, 98
Fowler, Flt Lt PR 92, 125
Fuller-Good, Gp Cpt J D 30, 34
Furious, HMS 36, 37

Galland, Gen Ltn A 83
Gaunce, Sqn Ldr L M 75
Gear, Flg Off A H 92, 112, 126
George, Sqn Ldr E 34
Gillies, Flt Lt J 78
Gillies, Flt Lt K M 43, 53, 54, 59, 60
Gilroy, Gp Cpt G K 112, 113, 124
Gilroy, Plt Off 124
Glorious, HMS 36, 37, 128
Gneisenau, 37, 80, 84
Godden, Flt Lt S 26
Goss, Flg Off C 57
Graf Spee 35
Grafstra, Flg Off J 30, 40
Gray, Gp Cpt C F 146
Green, Gp Cpt C P 77
Griffin, Flg Off P 126

Griffiths, Sgt A M 112

Hafner, Fw A 113
Haire, Maj J 132
Hardy, Flt Lt O L 101, 112, 122, 125
Harris, AM Sir Arthur 141, 142
Havercroft, Wg Cdr R E 57
Heath, Flt Lt 'Zulu' 30, 34
Hill, A M Sir Roderic 143
Holland, Sqn Ldr R H 57
Horner, Sqn Ldr C 23
Hughes, Flg Off T 126
Hugo, Gp Cpt P H 76, 112
Hunt, Wg Cdr D A C 48, 54
Hunter, W/OW 112, 125
Hussey, Flt Lt R J H 121, 123
Hyde, Sgt 'Lobber' 30

Igoe, Wg Cdr W 81-83, 86
Illingworth, Flt Lt P 71
Immelmann, Ltn M 11, 26

Jago, Flt Lt E H 28, 30, 31, 33
Jamieson, Gp Cpt P G 37
Johns, Cpt W E 13
Johnson, A V M J E 8, 10, 74, 136
Jones, Sqn Ldr C A T 40
Jupp, Plt Off A H 112, 123, 124

Kasserine Pass 123-125
Keefer, Wg Cdr G C 73, 141
Kendal, Plt Off J B 41, 61, 73
Kennard, Wg Cdr H C 40
King, Flt Lt E B 23-25
King, Plt Off P J C 43
Kingaby, Wg Cdr D E 57
Kingcome, Gp Cpt C B F 57, 89, 90
Kitchen, Flt Lt J 91
Krohn, Flt Lt I 120
Kynaston, Sqn Ldr 'Kyn' 144
Lardner-Burke, Wg Cdr H P 135, 145, 148, 151
Le Cheminant, Flt Lt J 92
Lees, A M Sir Ronald 101, 104, 111, 113, 118, 119, 127-129, 132
Leigh, A Cdre R H A 35, 37, 44, 45, 48, 53, 60, 63
Leigh-Mallory, A M Sir Trafford 82, 84
Le Petit, Sqn Ldr 'Tiny' 119

Le Roux, Sqn Ldr J J 77
Lewis, Plt Off H S 108, 112, 115
Lister, Sqn Ldr F W 113, 114
Lowe, Plt Off J 111

McCaul, Flt Lt M 122, 125
McKay, Sqn Ldr D N E 78
McNickle, Maj M 94
Malan, Gp Cpt 'Sailor' A G 9, 10, 48, 68, 69, 70, 78, 136
Malan, Plt Off G F 122, 126
Mannock VC, Maj M 95
Maridor, Cptne J 143
Marples, Wg Cdr R 75
Mather, Plt Off R J 43
Mills, Gp Cpt RS 36, 37
Montgomery, F M Lord 99, 123, 132, 133, 141, 147
Morris, Flg Off G 20 21, 23
Mortimer-Rose, Flt Lt E B 124
Mottram, Sgt A 111
Mungo-Park, Flt Lt J C 67

Nelson-Edwards, Wg Cdr G 101, 113

Omdahl, Sgt 79
O'Meara, Sqn Ldr 78
Orton, Sqn Ldr N 22, 71
Oxspring, Maj R 8, 23, 133

Parsons, Sgt C A 54, 59
Paton, Plt Off D 30, 32
Pattle, Sqn Ldr M T St J 10
Patton, Maj Gen G 129, 132, 133, 141
Perkins, Sgt FS 78
Pickering, Plt Off J H T 44, 42
Power, Flg Off R 30, 34
Preston, Mrs K 91
Prinz Eugen 80
Profumo, Maj J 132
Prytherch, Plt Off D J 92, 126

Rankin, Gp Cpt J E 78, 88, 94
Ratten, Wg Cdr J R 91
Reilley, Plt Off H W 58, 62
Rimmer, Lance 60
Rimmer, Flt Lt R F 40, 59, 60
Robbins, Plt Off R H 48
Robertson, Plt Off R J H 109, 121

Rommel, Gen E 99, 123, 124, 141, 144
Rook, Sqn Ldr M 98, 99, 100, 113
Roosevelt, Franklin D 151

RAF Airfields
  Acklington 92
  Ayr 92
  Biggin Hill 41, 48, 57-60, 63, 67, 68, 70, 78, 81, 82, 85, 86, 88, 91, 93, 94, 108, 119-121, 142
  Bône 101, 105, 106, 112, 119
  Brize Norton 22, 24
  Brough 20 21, 23
  Brussels 139, 150
  Coltishall 39, 42
  Cranwell 12, 35, 74, 108, 110, 135
  Crosby-on-Eden 71, 73
  Croydon 41, 59
  Deanland 146
  Debden 31, 32, 33, 41
  Detling 41, 148, 151
  Djidjelli 101
  Drem 93, 96
  Duxford 27-33, 35, 41, 53, 69, 73, 74, 120
  Eastchurch 41
  Exeter 70
  Gibraltar 99, 119, 135
  Gravesend 48, 56, 60, 62, 145
  Hartford Bridge 139, 140
  Hawkinge 38, 41, 55, 56, 76-80, 82, 83, 90, 96, 138
  Hornchurch 32, 33, 41, 91, 135
  Horsham St Faith 34, 37
  Kenley 41, 42, 45-47, 82, 84, 85, 90, 94
  La Marsa 130, 131, 132
  La Sebela 132
  Lympne 41, 61
  Maison Blanche 99, 100, 101, 113
  Maldegem 149
  Manston 38, 41, 120, 147, 150, 151
  Martlesham Heath 38
  Middle Wallop 41
  Morpeth 91, 92
  Northolt 41, 63, 82, 84
  North Weald 32, 33, 41, 146
  Perranporth 71
  Sidi Ahmad 130
  Souk El Arba 101, 104, 106, 115, 118,

125
Souk El Khemis 118
Speke 60, 66, 73
Tangmere 35, 41, 71, 74, 75, 86, 87, 93,
    94, 139, 140, 152
Thelepte 124, 125
Turnhouse 36, 37
Ursel 149
Warmwell 26
Watton 34
Westhampnett 73, 74
West Malling 53, 139, 142, 145

RAF and Allied Squadrons
1   120, 148, 151
12   13
19   28, 33, 35, 120, 121
41   75
43   100, 113, 114, 115
46   36, 37, 59
54   13, 35, 43
66   16, 27, 28, 30, 33, 34, 36, 37, 38,
         40, 42, 43, 45, 46, 52, 53, 54, 57,
         58, 59, 61, 62, 70, 71, 73
72   89, 90, 92, 93, 96, 100, 101, 102,
         103, 104, 105, 108, 110, 111, 112,
         113, 115, 118, 119, 120 ,121, 122,
         124, 125, 126, 127
74   48, 67-69
81   101, 119, 124
91   76, 78, 79, 85, 87, 138, 139, 143,
         146
92   48, 57, 59, 67
93   101, 113
99th   (USAAF) 134
111   94, 101, 113
124   89, 90
133   (Eagle) 89
152   101, 104, 106, 124, 125
222   93, 94, 96
225   101
232   96
241   111, 113
249   91
263   35-37
307th (USAAF) 94, 95
322   (Dutch) 138, 139, 140, 143, 146
331   (Norwegian) 152
504   34

602 94
611 91
421 77

Saint Omer 17, 91, 133
Scharnhorst 37, 80, 82, 84
Schneider Trophy 12, 136
Seagers, Flt Lt 'Gin' 143
Silk, Flt Lt F H 79
Sing, Wg Cdr J E J 101
Skinner, Flt Lt W M 67
Smith, Sgt A D 43
Smith, Sgt A R P 124
Smith, Plt Off K 112
Smith, Flt Lt L A 124
Smith, Wg Cdr W A 40, 59
Smuts, Gen Jan 17
Sollitt, Sgt S 126
Spurdle, Wg Cdr R L 79
Stephen, Wg Cdr H M 67
Stone, Plt Off G P 112
Storrar, Sqn Ldr J E 78, 148

Thomas, Wg Cdr E H 94
Tovrea, Lt E 95
Trenchard, M R A F Lord 29, 133
Tuck, Wg Cdr R R S 10
Turner, Maj S 117

Urwin-Mann, Sqn Ldr J R 135
Uxbridge 22, 32, 74, 84

Villa, Wg Cdr J W 57

Wade, Sqn Ldr T S 57
Walker, Gp Cpt P R 94
Ward, Sgt 31
Wardlow, Marmaduke 12
Willcocks, Sgt P H 48
Winskill, A Cdre A L 93, 96
Woodhall, Gp Cpt A B 35
Woods, Wg Cdr E M 90, 91
Wright, Wg Cdr A R 57
Wright, Sgt B 61